INTRODUCTION TO
GEOLOGY

DANTES/DSST* Study Guide

© 2019 Breely Crush Publishing, LLC

*DSST is a registered trademark of The Thomson Corporation and its affiliated companies, and does not endorse this book.

971103118143

Published by Breely Crush Publishing, LLC
10808 River Front Parkway
South Jordan, UT 84095
www.breelycrushpublishing.com

ISBN-10: 1-61433-612-1
ISBN-13: 978-1-61433-612-9

Printed and bound in the United States of America.

*DSST is a registered trademark of The Thomson Corporation and its affiliated companies, and does not endorse this book.

Table of Contents

 *Earth Materials*

Earth Materials are the various solids, liquids, and gases that make up the earth. Earth is primarily rock, water, and air. Rock is an aggregate or mixture of minerals.

Over 71% of the earth's surface is covered with water (oceans, lakes, rivers, streams, etc.), which is termed the hydrosphere. Most of this water is salt water found in seas, oceans, bays and some lakes. Fresh water is found in rivers, most lakes, and frozen in the polar ice caps. Pure water is a combination of the elements hydrogen and oxygen. These two elements make up about 96.5% of ocean water. The remaining portion is made up of dissolved solids. Sodium chloride is the most abundant of the dissolved solids which also include traces of magnesium chloride, magnesium sulfate, calcium sulfate, and other elements. Much of the water on the earth also contains elements which are pollutants.

The solid part of the earth's surface is called the lithosphere. This includes the seven major continents and all other landmasses. The landmasses are composed of rocks, minerals, soil, and sand. Rocks are made of one or more minerals. Soils are composed of particles of sand, clay, various minerals, tiny living organisms, and humus, plus the decayed remains of plants and animals. Sand is usually weathered rocks or shells.

Under the continents and oceans is the earth's crust which varies from 10 to 50 kilometers. The earth's crust is composed almost entirely of different combinations of the eight most common elements: oxygen (46.6%), silicon (27.7%), aluminum (8.13%), iron (5.00%), calcium (3.63%), sodium (2.82%), potassium (2.59%), and magnesium (2.09%). Oceanic crust consists mainly of basaltic rocks rich in the heavier common metals like iron and magnesium. Continental crust is composed of a variety of rock types, but the predominant rocks are granites which are rich in silicates (silicon and oxygen).

The layer below the crust is called the mantle. It is about 2900 km deep and is basically solid with some localized partial melting of the ferromagnesian silicates in the outermost layer. Below that are oxides of iron, magnesium, silicon and some minor elements which are all solids.

The core of the earth is divided into the outer core and inner core. The outer core is believed to be molten iron or a molten iron-nickel with some lighter elements like silicon, sulfur and oxygen. The inner core is thought to be solid iron or solid iron-nickel.

The atmosphere is the gaseous part of the earth which is referred to as air. Common gases include oxygen, nitrogen, and argon.

 Minerals

Rocks are composed of minerals and minerals are composed of elements. There are 88 elements found naturally. Oxygen is a negatively charged ion (anion) which combines with many different positively charged ions (cations) to form a variety of minerals.

There are over 3000 minerals in Earth's crust. Only about 20 minerals are common and 10 make up 90% of the earth's crust. Minerals are classified by composition. Minerals can be a single element like iron (Fe) or gold (Au) or a combination of elements. The major groups of minerals are metals (positive ions) combined with polyatomic ions such as the silicates ($SiO_4$4-), carbonates ($CO_3$2-), oxides (O2-), sulfides (S2-), sulfates ($SO_4$2-), and halides (H1-).

Minerals are naturally occurring inorganic substances, each with a unique crystalline structure. Minerals must adhere to five criteria. Each mineral must (1) be non-living, (2) be found in nature, (3) be solid in form, (4) have atoms which form a crystalline pattern, and (5) have a chemical composition within fixed narrow limits (proportions are always the same).

The key to understanding the structure of a mineral is to study the arrangement of its ions. That arrangement depends upon the electrical charges between the ions and their relative sizes. Minerals are distinguished from each other based on their chemical composition and crystalline structure, luster, hardness, weight (specific gravity), color, fluorescence, magnetism, solubility, cleavage, and radioactivity.

Two or more minerals can have the same chemical composition but different internal structures. For example, graphite and diamond are chemically the same, but their crystalline structures are dramatically different. Crystals do not normally grow evenly; one face grows faster than another so the final crystal looks nothing like the theoretical type for that mineral.

The crystalline structure may or may not be evident from the surface of the mineral, but it will be more evident based on its breakage (fracture or cleavage) which will expose its sides or crystal faces. Planes of weakness in the crystal lattice reveal themselves in the tendency for the crystal to split in a certain direction. For example, mica has silicate molecules arranged in flat sheets so it flakes away like the leaves of a book while calcite breaks apart into perfect mini-crystals. Both are examples of cleavage. However, some minerals fracture by breaking along an irregular surface. Fracture surfaces can be conchoidal or curved like the inside of a shell, hackly, splintery, or fibrous.

The number of possible internal arrangements is limited. There are six basic crystalline structures.

1. Cubic or isometric – 3 axes at right angles to one another and all of the same length. Examples: Iron pyrites (FeS_2), garnet

2. Tetragonal – 3 axes, all at right angles to one another, two of which have the same length. Examples: Copper iron sulfide ($CuFeS_2$), zircon

3. Hexagonal – 4 axes, three of which have the same length, at 120° to one another and at right angles to the fourth. Examples: beryllium silicate ($Be_3Al_2(SiO_3)_6$), quartz, calcite, dolomite, hematite

4. Orthorhombic – 3 axes, all three bases intersect at 90° angles and each are different lengths

5. Monoclinic – 3 axes, one not at right angles to the others, of unequal lengths. Examples: Pyroxene mica clay, arthoclase, gypsum

6. Triclinic – 3 axes, none of which is at right angles to any of the others, and all of which are different lengths. Examples: albite feldspar

Hardness is another method for identifying minerals. The Mohs Scale is used by geologists to assess hardness. It is a scale of "1" to "10" with "1" being the softest (talc) and "10" being the hardest (diamond). A simplified look at the Mohs Scale of hardness shows:

1. Talc   Fingernail can scratch
2. Gypsum
3. Calcite   Penny can scratch
4. Fluorite   Knife or glass can scratch
5. Apatite
6. Orthoclase
7. Quartz   File can scratch
8. Topaz   Quartz can scratch
9. Ruby, Sapphire
10. Diamond

The colors of minerals aid in their identification. Streak refers to the color of the mineral when it has been made into powder. A streak can be produced by scratching a piece of the mineral across the surface of an unglazed white ceramic tile (unless the mineral is harder than the tile). For example, pyrite which is known as "fool's gold" has a yellowish, metallic colored streak while feldspars have a white or pinkish streak.

Luster describes how the freshly broken (fractured) surface of a mineral reflects light. Many ore minerals have a metallic luster. Most of the silicate minerals have a glassy luster called vitreous. Resinous luster is similar to plastic in appearance. Silky luster (example: gypsum) is typical of minerals that are formed of thick masses of very fine hair-like crystals. Pearly luster looks like pearls.

Specific gravity is the weight of a mineral compared to the weight of an equal volume of water. The mass of the sample is taken. It is then immersed in a known (measured) amount of water and the measure of the water plus the sample is taken. By subtracting the original known amount of water from that, the amount of displaced water can be found. Dividing the weight of the mineral by the weight of the displaced water gives the specific gravity. A mineral with a specific gravity of 3 or more is noticeably heavy, so galena with a specific gravity of 7.6 would be "very heavy."

Bowen's Reaction Series

Bowen's Reaction Series describes the formation, or crystallization, of minerals as magma cools (i.e., as igneous rocks form). It summarizes the work of geologist Normal L. Bowen, who melted rocks and studied their properties to determine the characteristics of crystallizing minerals. Bowen determined that there were two different branches involved in the series: a discontinuous branch and a continuous branch. Because the two branches converge at lower temperatures, Bowen's Reaction Series is often depicted as a "Y," with the discontinuous branch on the left and the continuous branch on the right. The minerals forming at the highest temperatures and pressures are at the top of the Y, and those forming at lower temperatures are at the bottom of the Y.

The discontinuous branch is composed of rocks which contain silicates (silicon and oxygen combination), and heavy metals such as aluminum and iron. As the temperature becomes progressively cooler different types of rocks begin to form with different ratios of the components. Those forming at hotter temperatures contain a higher ratio of aluminum and iron. The order of the types of rocks is olivine, pyroxene, amphibolite and biotite. After which the discontinuous branch merges with the continuous branch.

Whereas in the discontinuous branch, where different types of rocks are formed, the continuous branch forms the rock feldspar with different concentrations of calcium (CA) and sodium (NA) with silicates. The rocks forming at higher temperatures will have higher concentrations of calcium, whereas those forming at lower temperatures will have higher concentrations of sodium.

Where the two branches converge is the formation of Potassium Feldspar (a potassium and silicate based rock), leading down to quartz which has the lowest crystallization temperature. The rocks which fall into this section include mica, quartz and granite.

Rocks, Ores and Gems

Minerals can generally be divided into two broad categories: the rock-forming minerals and the ore minerals. Since silica (SiO_2) is the most common chemical component of the earth, the most common rock-forming minerals are silicates. There are many types of silicates. Silicates can be SiO_4^{4-}, SiO_3^{2-}, $Si_2O_7^{6-}$, $Si_2O_5^{2-}$, or $Si_3O_8^{4-}$. The simplest is quartz which is pure silica. Metallic elements combine with silica. Magnesium-iron (ferromagnesian) silicates like olivine form a high proportion of the ocean crust while aluminum (nonferromagnesian) silicates such as feldspars form most of the continental crust. Carbonates (CO_3) like calcite and dolomite are also important rock-forming minerals. However, they are more easily eroded than silicates.

The ore minerals must contain a useful metal or nonmetal that is easily extracted. The feldspars of the continental crust contain aluminum but it cannot be easily extracted so they are considered rock-forming rather than ore minerals. On the other hand, some ores are pure metals such gold (Au) nuggets. Many ore minerals are oxides (O) combined with a metal such as magnetite (Fe_3O_4) or hematite (Fe_2O_3). Other ore minerals are sulfides (combined with sulfur) such as iron pyrites (FeS_2) or galena (PbS).

Gems are rare minerals which are considered beautiful as well as durable. The rarest and most valuable gems are called precious stones. These include diamonds, emeralds, alexandrites, and aquamarines. Semiprecious stones are not as rare, but are beautiful and durable. They include amethysts, zircon, garnets, turquoise, jade, malachite and opals. Most birthstones and stones used in jewelry are precious or semiprecious gem stones.

Rock Classifications

Rocks are classified into three main categories based upon how they were formed. Igneous rock is formed from magma crystallization. Igneus is the Greek word for "fire." Sedimentary rock is formed from fragments of preexisting rocks that are transported and deposited by wind, water, or glaciers. They can also be formed by the precipitation of solids or the evaporation of water from a solution. Metamorphic rock is rock that has been modified but not totally melted by high temperature and pressure.

By volume, more than two-thirds of the earth's crust is composed of igneous rock and about one-fourth is metamorphic. While sedimentary rock only makes up about 8% of the earth's crust, it is the most likely to be exposed at the surface.

Igneous Rocks

Molten rock is called magma. When molten rock pours out onto the surface of Earth, it is called lava. Most magma is formed at depths of about 60 to 200 kilometers below the surface where temperatures average 1400°C. Melting occurs near the surface during the uplift of mountains or during the formation of great cracks in the earth's crust. Magma forms near the bottom of the curst or within the upper mantle. Then magma moves upward into the crust, or it rises to the surface and flows out during volcanic eruptions.

When magma hardens, or crystallizes, igneous rocks are formed. Some magma reaches the surface and cools quickly to form extrusive rocks with small crystals. Some magma hardens beneath the surface where it cools slowly to form larger crystals. The slower the magma cools, the larger the crystals grow. Rocks with large crystals are said to have a coarse-grained texture. Granite is an example of a coarse grained rock. Rocks that cool rapidly before any crystals can form have a glassy texture such as obsidian, also commonly known as volcanic glass.

Igneous rocks are classified according to their composition and the way they formed. For example, gabbro and basalt have the same composition, but gabbro solidified inside the earth's crust while basalt formed outside the earth's crust. Basalt is found beneath all the ocean floors. Many volcanic islands, such as Hawaii, Japan, and the Philippines in the Pacific Ocean and Iceland and the Canary Islands in the Atlantic Ocean, were formed from basalt. Basalt is very fine-grained while gabbro is coarse-grained.

Sometimes fine-grained igneous rocks form so quickly that gas is trapped in them. Scoria has a mineral composition similar to that of basalt, but it is more than 50% holes. The other rock formed this way is pumice which is a natural glass with many holes. It cools so quickly that no visible crystals are formed. It is often so light it will float on water.

Texture helps in identifying igneous rock. The texture tells the story of how the magma cooled. Glassy texture means the magma cooled very fast and did not form crystals. Slower cooling produces a fine-grained texture of very fine crystals which can be seen in the sunlight with a magnifying glass. Coarse-grained rocks form with slower cooling. A pegmatitic texture means that the crystals are one centimeter in diameter or larger (they can be much larger). A porphyritic texture of coarse crystals in a fine-grained matrix indicates a change in conditions during the cooling process.

An old classification system was based on the idea that rocks are salts of some kind of "silicious acid" – silica or silicate by today's knowledge. It used the terms acidic, intermediate, basic and ultrabasic to denote the percentage of silica in a rock. An acidic igneous rock contains more than 66% silica; an intermediate igneous rock contains 52-66% silica; a basic igneous rock contains 45-52% silica; and an ultrabasic igneous rock contains less than 45% silica.

Silicate is a polyatomic ion with a negative charge which can range from two to six. This allows the silicate to combine with a positively charged ion of one or more metals. If it combines with potassium (K1+), calcium (Ca2+), or sodium (Na1+), a feldspar is formed. Orthoclase is the most common member of this family. Plagioclase feldspars are closely related as they all have very small crystals.

Iron and magnesium often combine singly or together with silicate to form mafic rocks. Olivine, amphibole, mica, biotite, and muscovite are possible resulting minerals. (Felsic rocks contain aluminum with silicate.)

Minerals crystallize over a broad range of temperatures and pressures. The weight of overlying rocks causes both heat and pressure. The decay of radioactive minerals also produces heat. As the magma approaches the surface, minerals crystallize out. The order in which they crystallize determines which minerals occur together. Some overlap of minerals occurs because temperatures vary throughout the body of magma even as it rises.

Some parts of the magma cool more quickly than others. Where magma is in contact with solid rock, cooling is faster than in the center of the mass. Small bodies of magma cool more quickly than large bodies. The composition of the magma also influences the rate of cooling.

There are two general types of magma. Basaltic magma comes directly from the mantle. This magma flows readily and forms thin layers that cover large areas, especially on the ocean floor. Temperatures of basaltic magma range from 900°C to 1200°C. Granitic magma is thick and stiff. Its temperature is generally below 800°C. Volcanoes of this material tend to be explosive, blowing out large amounts of ash and huge pieces of rock. Granitic magma generally forms just below the crust and contains crustal material that has been melted.

Intrusive Igneous Rock

Intrusive, or plutonic, rock includes any igneous rock that was formed below the earth's surface. Intrusive igneous rocks form as the molten material pushes its way upward through the rocks, cutting across or squeezing between them, and solidifying before reaching the surface. If such rocks cool slowly, they will be coarse and have mineral crystals big enough to be seen with the naked eye. If they cool quickly, they will be fine-grained. Sometimes the molten mass begins to cool slowly, crystals of one mineral begin to form and then the whole lot is thrust into another area where it cools quickly. This gives a porphyritic texture with big crystals in a fine groundmass.

Intrusive acidic rock shows large crystals, many of which are quartz. Acidic rocks tend to be lightly colored because of the presence of quartz. Granite is an example of an acidic intrusive rock and diorite is an example of an intermediate intrusive rock. Basic and ultrabasic rocks are dark. Gabbro is an example of a basic intrusive rock and peridotite is an example of an ultrabasic intrusive rock.

When magma hardens under the earth's crust, it forms irregular bodies of plutonic rock. These formations are classified by their size, shape and relationship to rocks around them. An intrusive rock formation that has an exposed surface of more than 100 square kilometers is called a batholith. Usually a batholith also extends vertically 10-30 km into the crust, but it is often hard to know how large they really are as they get thicker as you go deeper. Batholiths usually run parallel to the axis of a mountain range and have a domed roof. Batholiths are the largest structures of intrusive type rock and are composed of near granite materials; they are the core of several mountain ranges including the Sierra Nevada Mountains. One of the largest batholiths is the British Columbia batholith in Canada with an exposed surface of 2,000 km by 290 km.

A stock is similar to a batholith but less than 100 square kilometers. A stock may be an offshoot from an underlying batholiths.

Dikes are narrow, table-like bodies of igneous rock formed when magma entered a vertical or oblique fracture and hardened. The dike cuts across various layers of rock, but does not reach the surface.

In some cases, magma pushes its way between layers of sedimentary rocks. When the magma pushes the overlying rock to an arch, a laccolith is formed. The magma in a laccolith is very thick and does not flow easily; therefore, it pools and forces the overlying strata to create an obvious surface dome.

Sometimes magma squeezes between two rock layers and hardens into a thin horizontal sheet called a sill. The sill does not force the formation of an arch or dome but stays flat and horizontal.

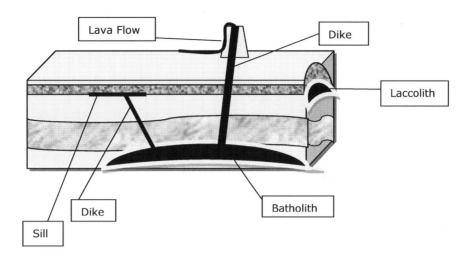

Extrusive Igneous Rock

Extrusive, or volcanic, rock includes any igneous rock that was formed at the earth's surface. For the most part this rock originated as lava that poured out of volcanoes. The lava cools quickly because there is no insulating earth cover. Therefore, extrusive rock often has tiny crystals and a fine-grained texture.

There are no ultrabasic extrusive rocks at the earth's surface. They are thought to be the main constituent of the mantle. Basalt is an example of a basic extrusive rock, andesite is an example of an intermediate extrusive rock, and rhyolite is an example of an acidic extrusive rock.

Felsite is another fine-grained rock and obsidian is a glassy rock produced by volcanoes. Other products that result from volcanic eruptions include volcanic ash, cinders, and dust as well as pumice and tuff. Pumice is actually a froth of volcanic material that has chilled and solidified with the bubbles intact. Tuff is a type of volcanic ash that has been partly consolidated.

Volcanoes are concentrated in particular narrow bands. The greatest concentration of volcanoes still active today (or recently extinct) runs around the rim of the Pacific Ocean. There is a whole line of volcanoes along the western coasts of South America, Central America, and North America. The line then goes out the Aleutian Islands, across to Russia's Kamchatka Peninsula and through the Kurilian Islands to the islands of Japan. The chain breaks into two parts with one swinging westward toward the Asiatic continent and down into the Philippines and the other eastward into the Pacific Ocean and toward the islands of Guam and Yap. This line then goes through New Zealand, the Solomon Islands, New Guinea, and the Malaysian Islands. The Ring of Fire circumscribes the Pacific Ocean.

There is also a Mediterranean Basin of volcanoes which stretches from Turkey through Greece into Italy and the islands of the Central Mediterranean. There is a string of volcanoes through central Africa. Iceland is really a large volcanic center. Many islands, including the Hawaiian Islands, in the Pacific Ocean and some of the islands in the Atlantic Ocean are either active or extinct volcanoes. All the oceans contain sea mounts which are drowned volcanoes and will be further discussed with ocean basins.

There are two types of volcanic activity: explosive and quiet flows of lava. At any given time a volcano may show one type or the other. It may do one for hundreds of years and then suddenly switch to the other for a few weeks or months or many years. The explosiveness of a volcano is dependent upon the amount of gas trapped in its lava and on the viscosity (ability to flow) of the lava. If the gases are held firmly within the lava and prohibited from escaping to the surface, large pressures build up and can only be relieved with an explosion. Explosive volcanoes tend to have lava with a high silica content. Less explosive volcanoes produce andesites and the least explosive produce basalts.

No two volcanoes are shaped exactly alike. However, there are three main shapes: basaltic flows, shield volcanoes, and composite cones. These reflect the nature of the magma and type of the volcanic activity.

A basaltic flow contains less gas and the gas it does contain can escape fairly easily to the air. Basaltic flows are very fluid and often flow as great sheets over large areas of countryside. The Columbia and Snake River plateaus of the northwestern United States are examples. The flows covered 400,000 square kilometers and range from a few feet thick to tens of feet thick.

When the lava erupts from a single central vent, they build up a mound that is broad and low. The slope is gentle (3° to 6°) and the lava bed contains mostly basaltic rock with only a few beds of cinders and ash. These are called shield volcanoes due to their very large, circular convex shape. Examples include the low cones of Iceland and the Hawaiian Islands.

A composite cone is formed because of the high pressure of gases trapped in the lava. These volcanoes are much more steep-sided (as much as 30° of incline in the top third) and much taller than the shield cones. They are fed by magma of higher silica content than the basaltic magma. The sudden release of pressure causes an explosive eruption that throws great quantities of fragmental material, pulverized pieces of rock, and much magma into the air and down the sides. It produces much more volcanic ash and cinders and huge clouds of smoke filled with ashes, cinders, rock fragments, and dust. Mount Vesuvius is an example.

A volcano may develop as a shield volcano during part of its history and as a composite one later. Mount Etna, on the island of Sicily, is an example.

A caldera is normally formed by the collapse of the top of a volcano. This collapse can be caused by a massive explosion that destroys the cone and empties most if not all of the magma chamber below the volcano. The cone collapses into the empty magma chamber forming a caldera. Normally the caldera is a wide (at least one mile wide), shallow depression which may fill with water and become a lake. Crater Lake, Oregon, is an example.

An inactive (extinct) volcano may have magma solidified in its pipe. This structure, called a volcanic neck, is resistant to erosion and today may be the only visible evidence of the past presence of an active volcano.

 # Sedimentary Rocks

The term sedimentary comes from the Latin word sedimentum which means "settling." Sedimentary materials include fragments of broken rock, mineral grains, and substances deposited from solution. Fossils of sea animals, plants, shells, insects, and other animals are common in sedimentary rocks. Sedimentary rocks are usually very recognizable in the field as they lie in distinct layers or beds. The analysis of the beds tells us much about the earth's history.

Fossils and sediments are clues to the past. Large, unweathered fragments of rocks suggest a rugged mountain source and mechanical weathering. Quartz grains suggest long transportation during which other materials were lost. Muds suggest deposition in a quiet body of water where only the finest sediment reached deep water. Muds also suggest complete decomposition in the source area.

The most abundant sedimentary rocks are shale, limestone, and sandstone. Shale accounts for over half of all sedimentary rock, and the three together account for 99% of all sedimentary rock. Shales are the basic, raw material for pottery, brick, tile and china. Oil shale is used as an energy resource. Quartz is the predominant mineral in most sandstones. Quartz sandstone is the raw material for glass.

Sedimentary rocks are classified as clastics and nonclastics. Clastic rocks contain fragments of rocks, grains of minerals, and crushed shells. Nonclastic rocks are deposited from solution or by organic processes. Biogenic nonclastic sedimentary rocks are composed of material produced by living organisms. The chemical nonclastic sedimentary rocks are those produced by inorganic chemical material being deposited on the floor of a sea or lake and then building up into a solid mass.

Clastic Sedimentary Rocks

Clastic rocks contain fragments of rocks carried by rivers, winds, waves or glaciers. They are generally deposited as the velocity of the transporting agent decreases. With the exception of glaciers, these agents drop their loads as their movement slows. Large, heavy pieces are dropped first, and as speed continues to decrease, smaller and smaller sized pieces are dropped. When glaciers melt, the rocks in them are left right where the glacier melted.

Clastic rocks are named according to the size and shape of their fragments. Conglomerates are mixtures of rounded pebbles of any kind and any size. Clay and sand grains can also be present. Breccia is similar to conglomerate except that its fragments are sharp, angular pieces. Breccias keep their angular shape because they have not been moved far enough, rubbed against enough other rocks, or been weathered enough to have their edges rounded off. The particles in conglomerates are usually greater than 2 millimeters (0.02 inches).

Sandstones consist of small grains of quartz, basalt, calcite, or even feldspar. These materials feel gritty and grains are easy to see. Beach and river sands usually are quartz grains. Black sand beaches of Hawaii are ground up basalt lava. (In the Bahamas and many places in Florida beach sands are shell fragments.) Siltstone is like sandstone but with much smaller grains which can be felt; however, they can only be seen with a magnifying glass. Clay is usually present in large amounts. The particles in sandstones are 0.004 to 2.0 mm (0.00015 to 0.02 in).

Shale is made of thin layers of clay fragments too small to be seen. Mica flakes, which are common in shales, give the rock surface a smooth, slippery feel. Shales are mud which has been pressed into fine layers. The particles in shales are less than 0.004 mm (0.00015 in).

When sediments are transformed into solid sedimentary rocks, the process is known as lithification. Lithification includes all the steps and processes by which a layer of rocky fragments or a bed of sand or a heap of seashells can become a sedimentary rock.

All clastic rocks undergo some kind of hardening process. Shale and siltstone become rocks by compaction. Mud balls show how easily clay can be hardened by squeezing. The weights of overlying materials compress and compact the deeper sediments. Compaction in nature occurs when mud or silt is buried and water and air are squeezed out. Tiny clay particles are pressed together so tightly that water cannot move through the rock. Shale is impermeable (does not allow fluids such as water to go through it). Siltsone, with a large clay content, also hardens with compaction. When siltstones, sandstones, breccia, and conglomerates undergo compaction, the fragments are pushed into the smallest possible space.

Some siltstone must go through cementation to become a rock. Waters carrying dissolved minerals move through the sediments, and silica or calcite is precipitated between the grains and fragments, cementing all the parts together. Spaces between sediments may be completely filled with cement. Sandstones and conglomerates usually have some openings left which are connected. The measure of the amount of void space in a rock is porosity. Such rocks are permeable and may contain water or oil while buried beneath the surface. Permeability is a measure of the interconnectedness of the void spaces.

Sometimes the water acts on the fragments and induces the mineral crystals in them to continue to grow until they become a single interlocked solid mass. This is called recrystallization.

Nonclastic Sedimentary Rocks

Nonclastic rocks are either chemically or organically (biogenically) formed rocks. The chemical sedimentary rocks can be precipitates or evaporites. Organic rocks are formed directly or indirectly from material that was once living.

Precipitates from solution occur when chemical reactions form a solid that settles out of solution. Calcite is the most common precipitate. It is found in caves and as cement in other rocks. Many beds of limestone also are precipitates.

Evaporites form when water evaporates, leaving its dissolved solids behind. Evaporites include calcite, rock salt, and gypsum. Often thick layers of salt and gypsum are deposited between layers of shale and limestone. New York, Michigan and Kansas have deposits of salt and gypsum.

Organic (biogenic) deposits result from life processes. Shells or bones of calcite or silica collect. The shells of small sea animals sink to the ocean floor when the animals die. Larger shells also sink to the bottom but may be broken into smaller pieces from the weight of the water and action of the currents.

Algae die and fall to the ocean floor also to become part of the mud. Sea worms eat the mud to get at the plant remains. The pellets they secrete as waste are about the size of a grain of sand, but are very common in limestone.

Corals, sea animals that secrete a hard covering of calcite around their bodies (exoskeleton), live in colonies in shallow water. They form reefs hundreds or even thousands of meters thick. As they harden, these reefs become limestone. Such limestone reefs are found off the coast of Florida, around many of the Caribbean Islands and Pacific Ocean islands and along the coast of Texas.

Chalk is a form of limestone that is composed of small pieces of animal shells and crystals of calcium carbonate pressed together. It is a soft type of limestone.

Plant debris such as trees, twigs, and ferns may be buried in a swamp or bog. Eventually this organic material becomes peat. With further burial, peat is changed to coal. The percentage of carbon increases as the volatile hydrocarbons and water are forced out of the deposit. Coals are ranked according to the percentage of carbon they contain. Peat, with the least amount of carbon, is the lowest-ranking; then come lignite, or brown coal; bituminous, or soft coal; and finally, anthracite, or hard coal, the highest in percentage of carbon. The higher the percentage of carbon, the cleaner the coal burns and the fewer pollutants it produces.

Nonclastics are named according to their composition. These rocks include limestone which is composed of calcite, flint or chert which are made of silica, rock salt from the mineral halite, and alabaster which is made of gypsum or anhydrite. Chemically formed nonclastics have crystals that are interlocking and so need no further hardening to be called rocks. Many of the crystals are large, but chalk, a kind of limestone, has crystals and shells only visible under a microscope.

Characteristics of Sedimentary Rocks

Ripple marks form on dunes or beaches. They look like small waves in the sand. Ripple marks formed by water or wind currents from a relatively constant direction have a gentle slope on one side and a steep slope on the other side. Wind or water carries the sand up the front slope, then drops it on the back side. The back side becomes steep compared to the front side. Ripple marks formed by waves have about the same shape on the front and back. Incoming waves push sand in one direction. Returning water pushes sand back again, keeping the ripple with the same slope on each side. Ripple marks show the direction of currents that flowed across the rock as it formed.

Mud cracks form along shores or in riverbeds where mud deposits are completely dried out from time to time. Sand may be blown into the cracks. Then the cracks are preserved even if covered with water at a later time. Mud cracks indicate periodic drying.

Concretions are features formed in the upper surface of certain rock layers. Concretions form when cementing material collects around a core which may be a bone or other fossilized material, a mudball, or a mass of sandstone. Concretions form in layers and may be centimeters to meters in diameter.

Geodes are hollow, ball-like bodies sometimes found in limestone. Quartz crystals grow inward from a hard outer rim of silica. The quartz may be colorless, smoky, or purple.

In dry climates, rock exposed at the surface is more likely to be weathered mechanically which produces sharp cliffs. In humid climates, chemical weathering is more common and creates a landscape with rounded features.

Chemical weathering describes situations in which the actual minerals within rocks are broken down through interactions with the atmosphere (air) and hydrosphere (water systems). Chemical weathering therefore changes the chemical composition of a rock over time. One simple example of chemical weathering would be acid rain.

The rocks that are most susceptible to chemical weathering are those which are not accustomed to the conditions on the surface of the earth, but which are formed within the earth and then later exposed. The more surface area a formation has, the faster chemical weathering will occur. The most important element in chemical weathering is water because it is involved in most chemical weathering processes. Because of this, warm tropical climates are the most conducive to chemical weathering of rocks. The heat acts as a type of catalyst in speeding the chemical reactions which break down the minerals.

A mixture of different sized grains in a rock indicates that the sediment was dumped rapidly. Grains of the same size indicate that the particles were sifted and sorted before being deposited. Because the sediments are moved by wind or water, the grain size and pattern of deposition indicate much about the area hundreds of years ago. The faster the wind or water moves, the larger the particles that are moved. Flooded rivers move very fast and can move very large boulders.

Sand and gravel are moved on and off beaches during major storms such as hurricanes. Dry sand is piled on beaches during wind storms. Whole sand dunes change location over time with wind movements.

Slow-moving wind and water can only move small grains. Mountain streams often leave gravel deposits when they reach flat ground. Sediments get carried into lakes and oceans. When they are carried out into deep water, they settle slowly to the bottom. The smallest grains, like clay particles, can remain suspended in standing water. Any movement of the water will move these particles.

Evaporites can form when a body of ocean water is cut off from the rest of the ocean or a river flows into a lake that has no outlet. When the water evaporates, the concentration of minerals increases because no water is carrying the minerals away. Eventually, the concentration of minerals becomes so great that they are deposited. The Great Salt Lake in Utah is an example of a lake where evaporites have formed because the lake has no outlet.

Sedimentary rocks are often layered, or stratified. The bedding pattern (layers called strata) of sedimentary rock shows the order of deposition. The oldest rock is usually at the bottom. The surface of each bed is essentially parallel to the horizon at the time of deposition, and in cross section, the beds expose a series of layers like those of a giant cake.

The thickness of the bed indicates the length of time during which those sediments were being deposited. A new layer indicates a change in conditions.

Although deposits are usually laid down in horizontal beds, some are created at angles to the horizontal. A bed laid down on the surface of a sand dune and some beds that build up on a delta are inclined. A special type of inclined bed is created if scouring (sudden washing with fast running water) occurs. For example, flooding or vast amounts of melting snow can cause a stream or river to increase its volume and velocity and carry sand and gravel from the bottom of the stream or river to another location. When the velocity and volume return to normal, the depression fills with new sediments which fill in from the edges. When the depression becomes filled and is even with the edges, a new horizontal bed will form on top.

A fresh-water river changes to brackish-water as the river nears the ocean. In an ocean, the marine environment changes from shallow water to deep water with different organisms growing in different environments. Therefore, as the environment changes, the nature of the sediments that are laid down also changes. The deposits in one environment will show different characteristics than the ones in a neighboring environment. The change in how the resulting sedimentary rock looks is called a change in sedimentary facies. The concept of facies is used in studying sedimentary rocks and the conditions that gave rise to metamorphic rocks.

In the western and southwestern United States, the bare cliffs and steep-walled canyons provide a brilliant display of colors in sedimentary rocks. The Grand Canyon of the Colorado River in Arizona cuts through rocks that range in color from gray, to purple, red, brown, buff, and green. The most important sources of color in sedimentary rocks are the iron oxides. Various amounts and combinations of iron produce red, pink, yellow, brown, green, purple, and black. Organic matter can contribute darkness and depth of color.

Metamorphic Rocks

Metamorphic rocks have, at some point, been changed either in texture or mineral composition. Any igneous or sedimentary rock can be changed (metamorphosed) into a metamorphic rock and any metamorphic rock can be changed into a different metamorphic rock (polymetamorphosed) through more pressure or a higher temperature. Therefore, the number of individual rock types in the metamorphic group is potentially greater than in the igneous and sedimentary rock groups combined.

Metamorphic rocks are formed by high temperatures, great pressures and chemically active fluids. The process by which the rocks undergo these changes is called metamorphism. Metamorphic changes include deformation by extreme heat and pressure, compaction, destruction of the original characteristics of the parent rock, bending and folding while in a plastic stage, and the emergence of completely new and different minerals due to chemical reactions with heated water and dissolved minerals. None of these processes can be directly observed.

Metamorphic changes require deep burial - to depths of 12 to16 kilometers beneath the surface. Temperatures at this depth range from 150ºC to 800ºC. While the rock is still solid, the original rock material undergoes a rearrangement of mineral grains, an enlargement of crystals, or a change in the chemistry of the rock.

Metamorphic rocks contain many minerals found in igneous rocks. They may also have minerals not found in any other kinds of rocks. The first metamorphic change is a rearrangement of mineral grains. Foliation takes place when minerals begin to line up in bands, or layers, when the temperature reaches 150ºC. As the temperature continues to rise, crystals tend to grow larger, and chemical reactions take place.

Sedimentary rocks form at the earth's surface. They contain the same elements as igneous rocks, but the elements are arranged in combinations that are stable at surface temperatures and pressures. During metamorphism, these low-temperature minerals are changed into minerals stable at high temperatures and pressures. Sandstone and shale are changed into quartzite and slate, rocks containing feldspars, amphiboles, quartz, and mica. Limestone is changed into marble.

Metamorphism is often associated with mountain building. As mountains rise, magma is forced toward the surface where it hardens into a mountain core. Metamorphic rocks surround the core for hundreds of kilometers. The rocks nearest the core are recrystallized. The amount of recrystallization decreases outward from the core. The rocks farthest from the core show foliation only.

Several kinds of metamorphism are associated with the mountain core. High temperatures make it possible for some ions to move from points of great pressure to points of low pressure. Crystals may be enlarged where pressure is low. Gases from the magma move through tiny rock openings and react with elements in the solid rock. New minerals are formed by this process called contact metamorphism. This kind of change occurs at temperatures around 800°C, near the contact between an igneous intrusion and layers of sedimentary or volcanic rock. Magma with a high percentage of water vapor carries rare elements that do not fit into the rock-forming mineral groups. These rare elements react with the surrounding rocks to form unusual minerals.

Metamorphism can occur only while the rock is solid because, when the rock reaches its melting point, magma forms and igneous activity begins. A rock can exist in the plastic state, a condition transitional between the brittle character of rocks at or near the earth's surface and the molten state of subterranean magma.

Metamorphic rock is classified in two ways – by the way in which it originated and by its type of texture. Metamorphic rock is formed in three ways. Thermal or contact metamorphic rock is formed at the margins of igneous bodies such as a dike of magma. The degree of closeness to the igneous intrusion into the preexisting, or "country rock" produces different conditions of heat and pressure and determines the type of metamorphic rock produced. Regional metamorphic rock undergoes much recrystallization and is formed when a large amount of it is under heat and pressure. This is the most common type. Dynamic metamorphic rock is formed when rock is broken and ground with little recrystallization. This type occurs in fault zones and from meteorite impacts. It is fairly rare.

In contact metamorphism all the elements of a rock may be replaced by other elements introduced by hot gases and solutions escaping from the magma. Farther away the replacement may be only partial. Contact metamorphism occurs in restricted areas called aureoles which seldom measure more than a few hundred feet in width and can be only a few millimeters wide. Aureoles are found bordering laccoliths, stocks, and batholiths. A great deal of recrystallization is caused by the heat of contact metamorphism.

On the other hand, regional metamorphism develops over extensive areas, often thousands of square kilometers of rock several hundred meters thick. Many new minerals are developed as rocks respond to increases in temperature and pressure. These include silicate minerals not found in igneous or sedimentary rocks. Regional metamorphism may be divided into zones: high-grade, middle-grade, and low-grade. Each grade is related to the temperature and pressure reached during metamorphism. The zones are identified by using certain index minerals as diagnostic keys. The first appearance of chlorite is the beginning of a low-grade zone, the first appearance of garnet is the beginning of a middle-grade zone, and the first appearance of sillimanite is the beginning of a high-grade zone.

Metamorphic rocks are classified into two groups based on their texture – foliated (leaf-like) rocks and unfoliated rocks. Foliated rocks consist of compressed, parallel bands of minerals, which give the rocks a striped appearance and a layered breakage (cleavage). Examples of such rocks include slates, phyllites, schists, and gneiss. Unfoliated rocks are not banded. They do not have a preferred orientation of breakage. Examples of such include quartzite, marble, and anthracite.

 # Foliated Metamorphic Rock

Rock that is foliated has a layered appearance, in which the crystals are oriented in only one direction. Foliated rocks may or may not show recrystallization. Slates have no recrystallization; gneiss is mostly recrystallized with only faint banding. Slates are farthest from the mountain core, so they are very fine-grained. Some deeply-buried slates may be formed from the pressure of overlying rocks. Banding in slates is extremely fine and can be seen only with magnification. Phyllite layering is almost as fine, but mica flakes make the phyllite surface shiny in contrast to the dull surface of the slate.

Schists are medium-grained rocks that show some recrystallization and definite bands. They are the most common metamorphic rocks. Layers of dark minerals, either biotite or amphibole, alternate with layers of quartz or feldspar. Schists may form from impure limestones, shales, or basalts.

Gneiss, a coarse-grained rock, looks like granite except for its faint layering. Sometimes the layers are so far apart it is almost impossible to tell whether the rock is a granite or a gneiss.

 # Unfoliated Metamorphic Rock

Unfoliated rocks do not have banding. They lack minerals for contrast because they are single mineral rocks which makes them homogeneous. They include marble, quartzite, and serperntine. All of these rocks are recrystallized. Marble is changed from pure limestone. It is harder than limestone and its crystals are larger. Quartzite forms from quartz sandstone in which sand grains are recrystallized. Serpentine is metamorphosed peridotite or basalt. Some serpentine has marble streaks which formed from an original rock containing calcium. The marble is white or light colored, but the serpentine is green. Neither the marble nor the serpentine forms bands.

Some metamorphic rocks are made up exclusively or predominantly of a single mineral type. They are monomineralic. Examples are marble and quartzite. Monomineralic rocks are either unfoliated or weakly foliated.

Most metamorphic rocks are composed of two or more minerals, so are called multimineralic. Usually, but not always, these rocks are foliated. Gneiss is an example. It is composed of quartz, orthoclase, plagioclase, and one or more ferromagnesian minerals.

A typical sequence of rocks – from unconsolidated sediment, through sedimentary rock, through different grades of metamorphic rock, depending on the depth in the crust at which different conditions are found is:

Mud at the surface
Shale (sedimentary) at 5 km
Slate (low grade metamorphic) at 10 km
Schist and some Garnet at 15 km
Gneiss (high-grade metamorphic) and the beginning of staurolite at 20 km
Hornfels and other rarer minerals appear at 25 km

The Rock Cycle

The surface of the earth is continually being created and destroyed, but that process is usually not visible in a person's life time or by the naked eye. Matter from the earth's crust is changed from one form to another but never lost. The rock cycle represents the alteration of rock-forming minerals above and below the Earth's surface.

It starts with the uplift of magma inside the earth as it oozes or spews onto the surface of the earth. If magma is extruded onto the surface, it is called lava. Cooling above the surface yields rocks with fine textures, while those that form from slow cooling beneath the surface typically have large crystals. When it crystallizes, it becomes igneous rock. Igneous rock may re-melt when exposed to intense heat to form magma again, or be changed into metamorphic rock.

Igneous rocks may also be exposed to weathering, erosion and deposition to form sediment. When that rock is exposed, it is continually bombarded by weather. Rain water soaks through the pores. Frost freezes the rock and the moisture in it, cracking the pores open. Acid dissolved in the rainwater reacts with some of the minerals. Sun-warmed air expands the rock while cold air contracts it. Falling rocks from above may chip off pieces. And so the exposed rock becomes rubble and dust.

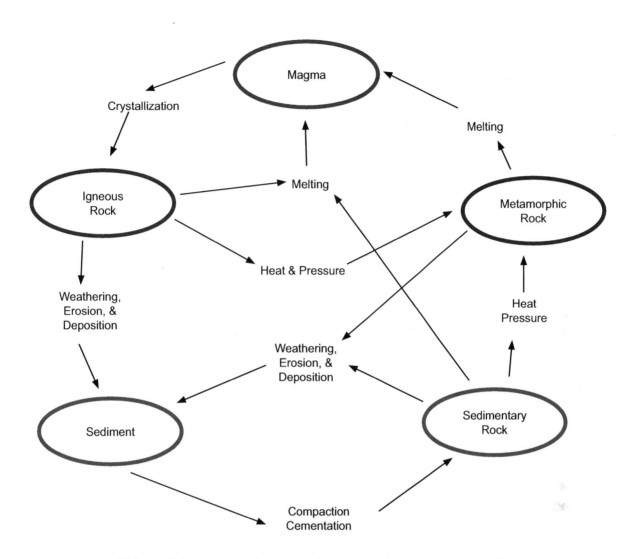

The rubble and dust are carried away by rain and wind. They may be swept down a river. They get deposited somewhere else where, over the years, they become lithified by compacting and cementing to become sedimentary rock. Sedimentary rocks may be broken down by weathering and erosion to be re-deposited as sediment, exposed to intense heat and/or pressure to be changed into metamorphic rock, or melted into magma by even more intense heat. Plate tectonic processes (to be discussed later) can also shove sedimentary rock into the mantle where it is re-melted into magma and recycled.

Metamorphic rocks are those that have been altered by exposure to heat and/or pressure. The pressure can be created by the weight of material lying above them. The collision of lithospheric plates creates pressure and heat that alters rock. If entirely melted, the rock material forms magma.

🎓 *Planetary Geology*

Planetary geology is the study of the planets and their moons (or satellites). Orbiting telescopes, space probes, and planetary rovers are giving vast amounts of new geological data each day. Photographs that come back to Earth each day raise questions as well as answer questions.

Mercury, the planet closest to the sun, has a surface that is characterized by refractory materials that can take heat. Its heavily cratered surface appears to have huge cliffs (scarps) that crisscross the planet. Radar data taken from the deep shade of north polar craters shows that there may be water ice at the poles. It is relatively small (4,880 km in diameter), has no known satellites, and has an eccentric orbit that varies from 46 million km (28.6 million miles) to 70 million km (43.5 million miles) from the sun. It also has the greatest temperature fluctuations of any of the planets in the solar system (from -183°C to 427°C).

Mercury's core is thought to be very similar to Earth's – a dense metallic, molten core surrounded by a silicate mantle and curst. The core generates a weak magnetic field. The planet's surface is pock-marked by impact events. Mercury has no plate tectonics, but huge escarpments associated with thrust faults give rise to the idea that the planet has shrunk.

Venus, farther from the sun than Mercury, comes closer to the Earth than any other planet. Due to a runaway greenhouse atmosphere, Venus is hotter than Mercury. Therefore, no life is able to survive or help mediate the atmosphere. Venus lacks satellites. However, Venus is very bright (can be seen in daylight) and can cast shadows at night. There appear to be no oceans on Venus.

Since the atmosphere of Venus is 97% carbon dioxide, scientists point to it as the ultimate example of the greenhouse effect. Its surface temperature is 800°F and its atmospheric pressure is 100 times that of Earth's. A nearly continuous acid rain known as virga contributes to Venus' inhospitability.

Apparently most of the surface of Venus is less than a half billion years old. Lava flows have covered over most of the older rock. However, the volcanic diversity is amazing. It varies from domes surrounded by concentric rings called coronae to flat-topped volcanoes referred to as pancake domes or farras to various small volcanoes. There are also smooth lava plains, elevated plateaus faulted into geometric tile patterns called tesserae and spiderlike features.

The surface geology of Mars is divided into two main regions: a region of older highlands south of the equator and a less ancient area of plains to the north. Parallel to and just south of the equator is the Valles Marineris, a huge canyon which is 4,000 km long and up to 6.5 km deep (the Earth's Grand Canyon is 804 km long and up to 1.6 km deep).

The southern highlands are heavily cratered. The northern plains are very low. Rising from the northern Amazonis Planitia is Olympus Mons, the greatest volcano in the entire solar system. It is a shield volcano 600 km in diameter and 26 km high (compare to Hawaii's Mauna Loa, Earth's largest volcano which is 120 km in diameter and 10 km high). Its great height is due to (1) the thin atmosphere and extremely limited hydrologic cycle and (2) the lack of plate tectonics on Mars.

Mars has a carbon dioxide-rich atmosphere, but more than 30% of it is lost to the CO_2 ice caps at both poles. There are always dust particles in suspension above Mars, so that it continually has a salmon pink tint. Dust accumulations deposited in the lee slope of crater rims indicate that winds on Mars blow with prevailing directions and carry and deposit sediments.

Many of the pictures taken by Pathfinder and Mariner 9 indicate that there may have been water on Mars. Sediments brought back by the Pathfinder landing rover have sulfide minerals unlike any on Earth. Pictures show collapsed ground, disrupted regions, meanders (like river meanders), delta-like areas, and craters that may have held water.

Jupiter has about 60 moons. Jupiter's largest moon, Io, shows recent volcanic activity. Another moon, Europa, appears to have a sea. Both Io and Europa are close enough to Jupiter to create powerful tidal forces. Ganymede is the largest moon in the solar system (even larger than Pluto or Mercury). Callisto is a heavily cratered moon due to impact battering.

Jupiter and Saturn have no surface geology because they do not have a solid surface or rocks. Their mass is liquid hydrogen. Jupiter's atmosphere is enriched with noble gases like xenon, krypton, and argon. It has been called a failed sun with a temperature of 24,000°C; however, it is not hot enough to sustain fusion reactions that would power a star. The pressure is so great, though, that it has continuous thunderbolts hundreds of times more powerful than any on Earth. Its liquid hydrogen sea has a metallic character that generates a magnetic field that is strong as far away as Saturn's orbit. Saturn's rings are not completely understood, but may be particles that represent the remains of captured bodies that are too close to become moons. They fall within the no-man's-land Roche zone where the tidal forces generated by Saturn's gravity would pull apart any attempt to aggregate.

Enceladus, one of Saturn's 35 moons, shoots an icy plume 1,000 km (620 miles) into the air above the surface. Hyperion, an oblong satellite of Saturn, has a spongelike texture consisting of radiating pores that make it resemble a giant floating block of pumice. Other moons of Saturn include Mimas, Tethys, Dione, Rhea, Titan, and Iapetus. Pictures from the landing on Titan of the European Space Agency's probe Huygens show channels with dark beds which contrast with the lighter terrain, a number of dendritic channels which appear to drain into a shoreline of a major river, and many round "rocks" which may be a type of ice.

Uranus and Neptune also lack a solid surface. Both have rings with Uranus' rings being nearly elliptical and Neptune's being circular.

Neptune's moon Triton has geyers. It also is the only moon in the solar system to rotate oppositely of all the others. This retrograde motion causes it to spiral inward toward Neptune. Triton is also the coldest object ever detected in the solar system.

Pluto was downgraded from a planet to a Kuiper Belt object in 2006 based on its inability to capture other objects in its orbital neighborhood. Other dwarf planets include Ceres and UB 313 which is also known as Xena.

Regolith is the most primitive type of soil – a layer of broken rock, soil and loose sediment – which has not yet undergone the processes that modify pulverized rock and transform it into soil. The entire process is unique to the Earth. Other bodies in our solar system including various planets and their moons and the Earth's moon develop regolith. However, they lack the hydrologic cycle and the catalytic activities of microbes that are found on Earth, so the soil stays in the regolith state forever.

Surface Processes

The processes that have shaped and formed the face of the earth continue all around us every day. Weathering, erosion, and mass wasting are the processes that form the fundamental principle of uniformitarianism. Weathering breaks rocks into smaller pieces or changes the rock's composition from one form to another, and the pieces are then moved downslope or by gravity by a process called mass wasting, or by erosion through running water, wind or ice.

 *Weathering*

The breaking down of rocks at or near to the earth's surface is known as weathering. Weathering breaks down these rocks into smaller and smaller pieces. There are two types of weathering: physical weathering and chemical weathering.

Weathering products include fragments of rock and chemically altered minerals. Some weathering products stay in place and form soils or loose sediment. Broken rock, soil, and loose sediment forms a primitive type of soil known as regolith which has not undergone the geochemical processes that transform it into soil. Some products are carried away by wind, water, or moving ice and deposited in a new environment. This process is called erosion.

Physical weathering, or disintegration, is the process by which rocks are broken down into smaller fragments without undergoing any change in chemical composition. Minerals may be separated along their faces. Physical weathering is mainly caused by the freezing of water, the expansion of rock, and the activities of plants and animals.

Frost wedging is the cycle of thawing and refreezing. This cycle causes large rock masses, especially the rocks exposed on mountain tops, to be broken into smaller pieces. Physical weathering or disintegration is important in the temperate zone because of the alternating of freezing and thawing. Water gets into cracks and pores in the rock. When ice forms, it widens openings and allows more water and snow to enter during the next thaw or storm. Piles of broken rock fragments at the foot of mountain slopes show that ice wedging is an important process in the mountains. This frost cycle is the most important factor in weathering (and erosion) in higher altitudes and latitudes.

In hot, dry climates the difference in temperature between day and night can have a destructive effect. Rocks expand in the heat and contract in the cold. When this happens to exposed surface layers, they tend to become separated from underlying layers. This is most obvious when the rocks are distinctly bedded, with planes of weakness parallel to the surface. When it happens on massive rocks such as granite, the result is that the rock erodes in curved slabs. The peeling away of the outer layers from a rock is called exfoliation. Rounded mountain tops are called exfoliation domes and have been formed in this way.

Sheeting is another kind of mechanical weathering which is especially important in granite masses formed deep in the earth. When overlying material is removed from the granite and it is exposed to low surface pressures, the rock expands. Cracks form parallel to the earth's surface, leaving thin sheets that break and slip very easily.

Animals burrow into the soil, leaving channels through which water and air reach greater depths – sometimes as deep as rocks when the soil cover is thin. Lichens, a combination of algae and fungi, grow on bare rock. Acids formed during their metabolism and decay aid in the breakdown of rock surfaces. In fact, lichens may be responsible for starting the weathering process of many hard rocks.

Tree roots follow cracks and expand them. Eventually a large piece of bedrock or exposed rock can be split open by a tree root.

Erosion is the inclusion and transportation of surface materials by another moveable material, usually water, wind, ice or animal (including people) movements.

The most important cause of erosion is running water. Streams, rivers, and tides are constantly at work removing weathered fragments of bedrock and carrying them away from their original location.

A stream erodes bedrock by the grinding action of sand, pebbles and other rock fragments. This grinding against each other is called abrasion. Streams also erode rocks by dissolving or absorbing their minerals. Limestone and marble are readily dissolved by streams.

Wind is responsible for much erosion in dry climates. When the wind picks up dry particles and hurls them along, the effect is sand-blasting of rocks they contact. More sandblasting takes place closer to the ground, so a resultant rock might appear like a mushroom with a tall, thin pedestal and a broad head. Another effect is polishing of rocks on three sides. Sometimes the wind-blown sand wears a rock away at a particular point and cuts it or topples the parts above the worn-away place.

People are major agents of physical weathering. Deforestation allows erosion of soil and exposes rock to weathering agents. Inappropriate farming methods destroy topsoil. In areas with a soft rock, well-worn footpaths can wear into the rock. And people quarry the stone to build buildings and roads. People are also responsible for the most potent agents of chemical weathering since pollutants cause much of the acid in rain and snow.

Chemical weathering is the breaking down of rocks through changes in their chemical composition. It is also known as decomposition. New substances are formed as the chemicals in a mineral dissolve or react with chemicals in the air or water. An example would be the change of feldspar in granite to clay. Water, oxygen, and carbon dioxide are the main agents of chemical weathering.

Because the water molecule is polar, it will pull apart or dissociate to form reactive ions of hydrogen and oxygen. The hydrogen can replace positive ions in the crystalline structure. This destroys the original structure and hastens decomposition of the rock.

Hydrolysis is the reaction of any substance with water. When water and carbon dioxide combine chemically, they produce a weak acid that breaks down rocks.

$$H_2O + CO_2 \rightarrow H_2CO_3$$

Granite is weathered when hydrogen ions replace potassium ions in feldspar. The weathered feldspar is transformed into the clay mineral kaolinite:

$$6\ H_2CO_3 + 2\ KAlSi_3O_8 \rightarrow Al_2Si_2O_5(OH)_4\ (clay) + 4\ SiO(OH) + K_2CO_3\ (soluble)$$

When the carbonic acid (H_2CO_3) reacts with calcite in limestone or marble:

$$2\ H_2CO_3 + 2\ CaCO_3 \rightarrow H_2 + 2\ CaHCO_3\ (soluble) \rightarrow 2\ H_2O + 2\ CO_2 + 2\ Ca^{2+}$$

Disintegration and decomposition work together in many instances to break down rocks. How quickly a rock is broken down depends upon the composition of the rock, the climate, and the presence of cracks or openings in the rock. Even the hardest of rocks eventually can be broken down.

Minerals in igneous rocks crystallize at different temperatures. The first minerals to crystallize are unstable at the earth's surface, and therefore, first to decompose. Iron-magnesian minerals decompose first, followed by plagioclase feldspars, and then orthoclase feldspar. Quartz hardly weathers at all.

Metamorphic rocks generally weather more rapidly than igneous rocks. Sedimentary rocks which form at the surface weather little. The exception is limestone which dissolves in surface waters. (Limestone found in deserts tends to be very weather resistant.)

Climate plays an important role in weathering. Chemical weathering is most rapid where moisture and warmth are present. Decomposition is rapid in tropical climates and during the summer in temperate zones. High temperatures, plentiful moisture, and decaying vegetation encourage chemical reactions. Humic acid, an acid added to the soil by vegetation, speeds up chemical weathering. In desert areas and polar regions, low temperatures and the lack of moisture keep decomposition at a minimum.

Cracks in rocks allow chemical decomposition to cover more surface area. Joints are systems of cracks that break rock masses into large blocks. Most uplifted rocks have such joints which allow weathering on all sides of a rock mass. Weathering eventually results in spherical rocks.

Uplifted limestone which is mostly calcite is highly vulnerable to chemical weathering. The weak acid of rainwater seeps along cracks and joints in the rock, dissolving it. The joints are opened up into wide gullies called grikes with blocks of limestone, creating a landscape that resembles a city of square buildings and roads. The upstanding blocks are called clints. When this action takes place underground, caverns and potholes are formed the limestone is re-deposited to form stalactites (from above) and stalagmites (from below) in them.

Many igneous rocks also weather like this. Gabbro and olivine are especially vulnerable. They will become so worn that the landscape appears to be littered with a collection of spheres, leading to the term spheroidal weathering.

New minerals formed by decomposition include clay, quartz grains, soluble forms of silica, carbonates, and limonite. Orthoclase weathers to form the clay and soluble silica of soil and to release potassium ions which are used by plants. Olivine, amphiboles, and pyroxene form iron oxide and soluble silica. Iron oxide provides color to the soil. Calcium plagioclases form clay, soluble silica, and calcium carbonate. The soluble silica becomes cementing material or it may later be precipitated as chert or agate. Limonite weathers to form the rust color found in some soils.

Clays are washed downward by rainwater but sand grains (usually quartz grains) are left near the surface. In humid areas soluble matter is removed in surface waters. In arid regions soluble matter stays in the soil. Desert soils contain gypsum, calcite, and salt minerals.

Soil is that part of the surface zone that has been altered by weathering, erosion and the processes of breakdown that include microbes and decay. Soil covers most land surfaces.

The thickness of the soil depends on climate and slope. Where plant life is abundant, soils are thick as decayed vegetation speeds up chemical changes in the rock. Soil formed in place is especially thick on gentle slopes if it has not been disturbed. Such deposits are at the foot of the Appalachian Mountains, in southeastern United States, and in the Pacific Northwest. Soils and the underlying broken bedrock are about 150 meters deep. In the northern U. S. and Canada, the glaciers removed all the soil, and thick soils have not had time to form.

Soils are thin in arid regions, in prairie areas where winds are strong, and in mountainous regions. Winds carry away the soil if no plant life is present to hold it in place. Dust storms in the 1930s removed fertile soil from the Great Plains area. Soil also is carried away by rain or gravity in mountainous regions. In polar regions, weathering is very limited and soils are present only if lichens and mosses can grow.

Soils are divided into three classes according to their texture. These classes are sandy soils, clay soils, and loamy soils. Sandy soils are gritty, and their particles do not bind together firmly. Sandy soils are porous- water passes through them rapidly. Sandy soils do not hold much water.

Clay soils are smooth and greasy, their particles bind together firmly. Clay soils are moist and usually do not allow water to pass through easily. Loamy soils feel somewhat like velvet and their particles clump together. Loamy soils are made up of sand, clay, and silt. Loamy soils holds water but some water can pass through.

In addition to three main classes, soils are further grouped into three major types based upon their composition. These groups are pedalfers, pedocals, and laterites.

Pedalfers form in the humid, temperate climate of the eastern United States. Pedalfer soils contain large amounts of iron oxide and aluminum-rich clays, making the soil a brown to reddish brown color. This soil supports forest type vegetation.

Pedocals are found in the western United States where the climate is dry and temperate. These soils are rich in calcium carbonate. This type of soil supports grasslands and brush vegetation.

Laterites are found where the climate is wet and tropical. Large amounts of water flows through this soil. Laterites are red-orange soils rich in iron and aluminum oxides. There is little humus and this soil is not very fertile.

Oxidation is also known as rusting. It occurs when oxygen combines with iron to form iron oxide. Oxidation also occurs with sulfide minerals.

Sulfide minerals are often associated with coal deposits. If the sulfides in the waste piles (after the coal has been removed) become weathered, sulfuric acid is produced. This acid, known as mine acid, can dissolve and run into streams and groundwater which spoils the water and makes it unfit for organisms to live in and animals and humans to drink.

Ions that are in solution as a result of chemical weathering of rock are carried into the underground water supply, creating what is known as hard water. Hard water causes problems in cleaning because the ions bind with soap in such a way as to render it useless. Water softeners contain chemicals that remove or replace those ions with ones that do not bind with soap in that way.

Mass Wasting

Weathering alone does not produce significant changes in the structure of the landscape. Erosion and mass wasting are responsible for most of the major changes.

Mass wasting is the downslope movement of rock and soil under the influence of gravity. Erosion has to do with the movement of rock and soil by water, wind or ice.

The angle of repose is the angle at which loose material (gravel, sand, soil) sets at rest which is typically 25° to 40°. If a slope is artificially over-steep (such as in a road cut or excavation), the material becomes unstable and begins to move downslope.

Water is important in the process. It adds weight which makes the materials unstable. It also lubricates the materials. And it gives the materials a mode of movement.

If water is between the grains of the material and pressure is applied – more material or more water – the water moves. This is called pore pressure.

Some types of material, for example some clays, swell when they are wet and shrink when they are dry. This causes soil instability and leads to mass wasting.

Mass wasting usually needs a trigger or a series of triggers. Undercutting a slope (as for a roadbed), overloading a slope until it cannot support the weight, vibrations from earthquakes or explosions, or the addition of volumes of water from heavy rains or masses of melted snow serve as triggers. While most of mass wasting is seen in hilly or mountainous areas, it is also common along shorelines.

Mass wasting is classified on the basis of the moisture content of the moving mass and the relative speed of its movement. There are seven types of mass wasting, five are rapid movements and two are slow movements. The rapid movements include rock falls, slumps, rockslides or debris slides, debris flows or mudflows, and earthflows. Creep and solofluction are the two types of slow movement mass wasting.

Rock falls are seen in mountainous areas. Any detached pieces of rock may free fall directly downward or may bounce or roll down a slope. These rocks can become detached as a result of the freeze-thaw cycle or the loosening action of plant roots or some action by humans. The piece or pieces may break and fall quickly or they may already be broken and suddenly become an unstable overburden and fall.

Slumps are sometimes the result of grading soil too steeply. They are often seen along roads, especially interstates. Slumps involve a mass of soil or soil and other materials sliding along a curved, rotational surface (think of a spoon bowl). The result is a small, crescent-shaped cliff or scarp at the upslope end. The bottom or toe of the slump is a flow. Slumps often occur where resistant rock overlays weak rock.

Rockslides are also known as debris slides or landslides. They occur when blocks of rock or masses of unconsolidated materials slide down a slope. Frequently they are triggered by melting snow, heavy rain, or earthquakes. They can be very destructive as huge quantities of material can be moved in minutes, covering an entire community without warning.

Debris flows (or mudflows) most often occur in volcanic areas. Another name for them when associated with volcanoes is lahars. They generally follow established drainage patterns or valleys.

An earthflow usually forms in a humid area on a hillside or at the toe of a slump and occurs after a heavy rain or melting snow. The rate of movement varies from less than one millimeter a day to several meters a day, but it is often long-lived (days to years). It usually occurs where the materials include clay and silt.

A creep is a slow, downhill movement of soil. It is so slow that you cannot tell it is happening until you realize that tree trunks are curved at the base or that various long-term things like fence posts, utility poles or tombstones are all tilted. Eventually they and any walls or fences will be broken or overturned. Creep can occur as a result of freezing and thawing. Freezing water in the soil elevates sand grains as the soil expands. Then the grains drop vertically to a site slightly downslope during the thaw.

Solifluction occurs in areas underlain by permafrost. It occurs in the active surface layer that thaws in the summer.

Hydrologic Cycle

Water continually circulates at the surface of the earth. It evaporates from oceans into the atmosphere. As clouds, it drifts over land where it condenses and falls as rain or snow. Then it runs off the continents as rivers and streams or it soaks through the soil and rocks. Eventually it reaches the ocean again. The water that soaks into the earth can be drawn up into plants where it evaporates from the leaves and goes back into the atmosphere. The water in the rivers and lakes has some evaporation as well. The whole process is called the water cycle or hydrologic cycle.

Water that falls to Earth in the form of rain, snow, sleet, and hail is called precipitation. Precipitation is part of a continuous process in which water at the Earth's surface evaporates, condenses into clouds, and returns to Earth. This process is termed the water cycle. The water located below the surface is called groundwater.

The impacts of altitude upon climatic conditions are primarily related to temperature and precipitation. As altitude increases, climatic conditions become increasingly drier and colder. Solar radiation becomes more severe as altitude increases while the effects of convection forces are minimized. Climatic changes as a function of latitude follow a similar pattern (as a reference, latitude increases as you move either north or south from the equator). The climate becomes colder and drier as the distance from the equator increases. Proximity to land or water masses produces climatic conditions based upon the available moisture. Dry and arid climates prevail where moisture is scarce; lush tropical climates can prevail where moisture is abundant. Climate, as described above, depends upon the specific combination of conditions making up an area's environment. Man impacts all environments by producing pollutants in earth, air, and water.

Streams and Rivers

Rivers pass through three stages – youth, maturity, and old age. Each river is different. Some pass through the stages very slowly over thousands of years. Some seem to skip a stage. Others pass through one stage quickly and get stuck in another for hundreds of years. Even in the course of going through a stage, the river will change character as it wears away mountains or builds up plains or delta.

Most rivers begin in mountainous regions. Rain and melting snow causes heavy runoff on the steep slopes. The land which is drained by a river or stream is called its watershed or drainage basin. The runoff cuts small channels in the earth as it flows. Channels join together to form larger channels. And the channels begin to cut into the earth and to pick up small rocks and debris. The larger channels join to form streams which join to form a river. The channels to streams and streams to river pattern appears like the branches and trunk of a tree, so are called a dendritic drainage pattern. More and more rocks, soil and debris are swept away with the water.

A radial drainage pattern occurs when streams flow outward in several directions from an upland area. This can be seen on a volcano or where there is a dome of sedimentary rock such as beds that have heaved up over a laccolith. If the original rock eventually erodes, the rivers continue on the courses they have used since they were young. This lack of respect for the underlying geology is known as superimposed drainage.

Sometimes the strata are composed of hard rock interbedded with softer rock such as layers of sandstone and shale. The soft rock erodes first. The river follows the outcrop of the softer rock and flows parallel to it. As a result, a trellised drainage pattern occurs with the streams following the grain of the landscape (called the strike). They are connected by main streams running at right angles to them.

Sometimes the headwaters (beginning of the stream) will erode back, meeting up with another stream. When this occurs, one will abandon its original channel and combine with the other, forming a river capture.

During the youthful stage, the river is constantly eroding rocks, allowing exposures and cross-sections to be seen. It is full of splash and vigor, forming waterfalls and rapids. A youthful river can drop quite steeply over a short distance. The force and speed of the water forms deep gullies. Much rocky debris can be picked up and carried by the strong current. This causes the river to often be muddy.

A young river wears away bedrock and exposes fossils. It creates a steep-sided V-shaped valley. It can cut deeply into and through many layers of rock during this stage, forming a deep, steep canyon. The immature, or young, river covers almost the entire valley floor. Because of the force of the water, large pieces of rock as well as smaller rock and masses of sediment can be carried many miles by a young river.

As a river matures, rock at the upper side of a waterfall or rapid becomes eroded. The rock being carried by the river creates abrasion on the rock of the riverbed, smoothing all the rock involved and taking off all the edges. The amount of drop lessens. And the riverbed widens. Spring flooding occurs, widening the valley. Trees may be washed downriver during flooding. Those trees may have rocks intertwined in their roots. The area around the river becomes broader and flatter. The river becomes more curved and winding and forms loops called meanders. The flow of water slows down, so the erosion slows down.

Material is still removed at the outside of each curve and deposited on the inside of the curve, but the size particles are smaller and the distance of travel is much less. Deposited debris is more evident than bedrock. Wherever there is slowing, there is more deposition than erosion. The bluffs of the valley may be cut down to the native rock, but they may be overgrown with brush and trees.

With further aging, the landscape around the river becomes more and more worn down. It has made a progression from mountainous to rolling to gently rolling to basically flat. Eventually it becomes a peneplain, meaning "almost a plain." Peneplains usually are not much above sea level. Hills of rock that have resisted weathering and erosion on the peneplain are called monadnocks.

There are times when a mature river is in an area that is uplifted. The river will again cut down into its bed. The result is a gorge that meanders called an incised meander.

The best known example is the Brahmaputra River which starts in China, cuts south through the Himalayas to India and then through Bangladesh to the Indian Ocean. It appears to have drained the Asian continent before the Himalayas were uplifted by a tectonic plate collision. This is a phenomenal example of superimposed drainage.

A river that is in old age is weak and slow-moving. It seldom causes erosion of rock, but continues to carry soil and sediment and deposit it. When flooding occurs, debris and sediment is deposited throughout the valley. Banks called levees develop. Loops and islands are formed as part of the river bypasses a meander. Rivers moving down out of mountains or hills typically do so in a straight fashion; however, once they reach flatter ground they have a tendency to meander back and forth in random curved patterns. This generates a process of erosion and subduction at the curving points of the river. Minerals will be deposited and build up on the inside of the curve, and the water will further erode the outside of the curve. When a river meanders in a loop or horseshoe shape, therefore, eventually the erosion process will cut through the center so that the river no longer goes all the way around, but goes straight through and cuts off the outer loop. The resulting independent body of water is referred to as an oxbow lake, due the curved shape that it will have.

On both sides of a mature river or stream are flat areas called floodplains. Because that is the area of overflow during flooding, the river deposits rich sediment (alluvium) and soil in floodplains. As a result of repeated flooding, the soil of floodplains is rich and fertile. This makes them rich farming areas, but areas that are subject to being washed out in the event of heavy rains – even if the rains are upstream. If there is frequent flooding, marshes and water meadows may result. Marshes are wet grasslands; swamps are waterlogged forests.

Where a river flows into the ocean is its mouth. The river's speed decreases as it flows into a lake or ocean, so the river gets wider. Both the slower speed and the increased width cause the river to dump large amounts of the sediment it is carrying. This forms a delta. Deltas can be very large as in the case of the Mississippi River delta. In such a case, the coastal area is increased by hundreds of square kilometers.

As the river's fresh water becomes mixed with the ocean's salt water, salt marshes often develop. An estuary is an area formed at the mouth of a river where river currents interact with ocean tides. Estuaries are rich habitats for many living organisms and animals. One type of estuary (example: the Chesapeake Bay) is formed when seawater swamps the river because the ocean level rises. Another type (example: Waddansee estuary in the Netherlands) is formed when the continuous action of waves builds sand up across the mouth of a river and traps river water behind it. A third type, the fjord seen in Norway and Alaska, forms when rivers end in deep areas of water that are partially isolated from the sea. And finally, earthquakes and volcanoes create a low-lying estuary area in a coastline with only a narrow opening to the sea such as is seen with the San Francisco Bay.

The Nile River in Africa is the longest river in the world at 6,670 kilometers. The Amazon River in South America is the second longest, but because it is a younger river, it carries more water than any other river in the world.

Lakes

Lakes are inland bodies of water. They may be either salt water or fresh water. Lakes need a consistent supply of water, usually from river drainage. They may or may not have a method of drainage. The Dead Sea has no drainage. All the lakes in the world make up only 0.05% of the world's total volume of water. In terms of geological time, lakes are considered transient and temporary. They can disappear if more water flows out than flows in. New ones can be formed.

Lakes form in nondraining depressions or basins whose outlets are above the lowest part of the depression. Many lakes are the result of glacier action. During ice ages, glaciers gouge and scour depressions in the bedrock. These depressions provide nondraining basins for the meltwater to collect. Glaciers also produce dams by depositing debris across the drainage paths of streams.

In areas of low precipitation and high evaporation, some substances can become concentrated in lakes. Water that flows into the lakes often carries dissolved minerals. If the mineral is sodium chloride, saltwater lakes form. Dissolved sulfates create bitter lakes, carbonates crate alkali lakes, and borates create borax lakes. In North America most salt lakes are found in the great Basin area of the western U.S. because there are no drainage outlets to the ocean. The only escape for water is through evaporation.

The world's largest network of freshwater lakes is the Great Lakes. Since they are freshwater, they are not seas as the terms sea and ocean refer to saltwater bodies of water. The largest freshwater lake by volume is Lake Baikal in southern Siberia. It is 7 kilometers deep (the Grand Canyon is 1 km deep) and contains 20% of the world's fresh water.

Groundwater

Precipitation that soaks into the ground through small pores or openings becomes groundwater. Gravity causes groundwater to move through interconnected porous rock formations from higher to lower elevations. The upper surface of the zone saturated with groundwater is the water table. A swamp is an area where the water table is at the surface. Sometimes the land dips below the water table and these areas fill with water forming lakes, ponds or streams. Groundwater that flows out from underground onto the surface is called a spring.

Permeable rocks filled with water are called aquifers. When a layer of permeable rock is trapped between two layers of impermeable rock, an aquifer is formed. Groundwater fills the pore spaces in the permeable rock. Layers of limestone are common aquifers. Groundwater is collected in reservoirs.

Groundwater provides drinking water for 53% of the population in the United States. Much groundwater is clean enough to drink without any type of treatment. Impurities in the water are filtered out by the rocks and soil through which it flows. However, many groundwater sources are becoming contaminated. Septic tanks, broken pipes, agricultural fertilizers, garbage dumps, rainwater runoff, and leaking underground tanks pollute groundwater. Toxic chemicals from farmland mix with groundwater. Removal of large volumes of groundwater can cause the collapse of soil and rock underground, causing the ground to sink. Along shorelines, excessive depletion of underground water supplies allows the intrusion of salt water into the fresh water field. Then the groundwater supply becomes undrinkable.

Groundwater usually contains large amounts of dissolved minerals, especially if the water flows through limestone. As groundwater drips through the roof of a cave, gases dissolved in the water can escape into the air. A deposit of calcium carbonate is left behind. Stalactites are icicle-like structures of calcium carbonate that hang from the roofs of caves. Water that falls on a constant spot on the cave floor and evaporates leaving a deposit of calcium carbonate builds a stalagmite.

Large features formed by dissolved limestone (calcium carbonate), include sinkholes, caves, and caverns. Sinkholes are funnel-shaped depressions created by dissolved limestone. Many sinkholes started life as a limestone cavern. Erosion weakens the cavern roof causing it to collapse, forming a sinkhole.

Glaciers

A glacier is a large, slow-moving river of ice, formed from compacted layers of snow. Gravity is the force that moves a glacier. Glacial ice is the largest reservoir of fresh water on Earth, and second to oceans as the largest reservoir of total water.

Geologic features created by glaciers include end, lateral, ground and medial moraines that form from glacially transported rocks and debris; V-shaped valleys changed to U-shaped valleys, often with cirques at their heads; and the glacier fringe which is the area where the glacier has recently melted into water.

After an episode of glaciations, the glaciers melt and retreat and leave behind piles of unsorted rock debris known as till. A drumlin is an oval-shaped mound of till. Its tip points in the direction that the glacier was moving. The first thing that happens to regolith or till is the leaching out of a variety of ions as water interacts with the mineral surfaces in the rock.

A unique part of the hydrological system, glaciers cause a number of distinctive landscape features. One example is the striations that are left behind in areas where glaciers have been. Because large rocks and other sharp, heavy objects are trapped in the glacial ice, as a glacier moves through an area they will leave long streaks in the ground, all running in the same direction. These are referred to as striations.

Another landscape feature which results from glaciers is a U-shaped valley. When a river cuts through an area, the valley that results will end in a point, like a V. However, glaciers push through canyons and erode them into a U-shape.

A moraine is a glacially-formed accumulation of unconsolidated debris which could have been plucked off the valley floor as the glacier advanced or could have fallen as a result of frost wedging. The debris can be of any size -- as fine as flour all the way to large boulders. However, it is usually angular, showing little or no abrasion or wearing. Rocks can be carried great distances by glaciers. Studying moraines helps scientists to determine where a glacier started and what path it may have taken.

Lateral moraines are parallel ridges of till (unsorted rock of varying sizes) deposited along the sides of an alpine glacier. Lateral moraines are deposited on top of the glacier due to frost shattering of the valley walls. Lateral moraines stay tall because they protect the ice under them from melting. Medial moraines form when the lateral moraines of two glaciers merge together. They, thus, form a ridge down the center of the combined glaciers.

Ground moraines are till-covered areas with irregular topography and no ridges. They often appear as gently rolling hills or plains. The till of these areas accumulated under the ice (by lodging there) and was deposited as the glacier retreated. End moraines (or terminal moraines) are debris deposited at the snout or end of the glacier and show the shape of the glacier's terminus. Glaciers act like a conveyor belt carrying debris from the top of the glacier to the bottom where it deposits the debris as the ice melts. End moraine size and shape is determined by how long the glacier stays in one place and if it advances or retreats after that.

A temperate glacier is at the melting point throughout the year. The ice of polar glaciers is always below the freezing point so the only mass loss is through sublimation (direct ice to atmosphere evaporation). Sub-polar glaciers have a seasonal melting time near the surface with some internal drainage.

The dry snow zone is a region of the glacier where no melting occurs, even in the summer. The percolation zone is an area with some surface melting. It is called percolation because the meltwater percolates into the snowpack and is refrozen. The wet snow zone is the region where all of the snow deposited since the end of the previous summer has been raised to 0ºC. And the superimposed ice zone is where meltwater refreezes forming a continuous mass of ice.

The accumulation zone is the upper part of a glacier which receives most of the snowfall. It accounts for 60-70% of the glacier's surface area. The depth of the ice of this part of the glacier exerts a downward force which causes deep erosion of rock. After the glacier is gone, this part of the glacier leaves large bowl-shaped depressions called cirques.

The other end of the glacier is its foot or terminus. This is the deposition or ablation zone, an area where there is more melting than accumulation, so all the sediment is deposited. Where the glacier thins to nothing is the ice front.

Melting ice forms a stream, called a meltwater stream, that flows from the end of the glacier. This stream carries away sand and gravel which are deposited in long, trainlike deposits called valley trains. The meltwater may also form small lakes and ponds near the glacier. Sediments deposited by rivers of glacial meltwater in a fan-shaped area ahead of the terminal moraine form very fertile areas called outwash plains.

Glacial striations are long, linear rock scratches that follow a glacier's direction of movement. Chatter marks are divots in the rock. Glacial erratics are rounded boulders that were left by a melting glacier. These may be seen perched precariously on exposed rock faces of a very different type of rock after glacial retreat.

Alpine Glaciers

Alpine glaciers are found in mountain terrains. The smallest alpine glaciers form in mountain valleys and are called valley glaciers. Larger glaciers, called ice caps, can cover an entire mountain, a mountain chain, or a volcano. Ice caps feed outlet glaciers which are extensions of ice into valleys below. Alpine glaciers move down a mountain by gravity.

Continental Glaciers

Continental glaciers cover large areas that are not necessarily mountains but can include mountains. Antarctica and Greenland are the only places where continental glaciers exist today. The volume of ice in these sheets is so large that if the Greenland ice sheet melted, it would raise the sea levels around the world by 6 meters (20 feet) and if the Antarctica sheet melted, it would raise sea levels 65 meters (210 feet).

Plateau glaciers cover some plateaus and high-altitude areas. They resemble continental glaciers but on a much smaller scale. Plateau glaciers are found on Iceland, large islands in the Arctic Ocean, and from southern British Columbia to western Alaska.

Tidewater glaciers are glaciers that flow into the sea. As the ice reaches the sea, pieces break off, or clave, forming icebergs. Since most tidewater glaciers calve above sea level, a huge splash occurs when the iceberg strikes the water. If the water is deep, glaciers can calve underwater, causing the iceberg to suddenly seem to explode up out of the water. One of the longest tidewater glaciers is the Hubbard Glacier of Alaska with a calving face over 10 kilometers long.

 Ice Ages

An ice age is a period of long-term reduction in the temperature of Earth's climate which results in an expansion of the continental glaciers and alpine glaciers. At least three ice ages have left evidences over the earth. There are three types of evidence: geological evidence such as rock scouring and scratching, moraines, deposition of till and glacial erratic, and valley cutting; chemical evidence such as variations in the ratios of isotopes in sedimentary rock; and paleontological evidence such as changes in the distribution of fossils.

The earliest ice age appears to have occurred 2.7 to 2.3 billion years ago during the Paleogne Period. It is known as the Huronian Ice Age. The earliest, well-documented ice age occurred 850 to 630 million years ago (during the Proterozoic Period) and probably produced Snowball Earth, an ice cover over the entire globe. A minor ice age probably occurred from 460 to 430 million years ago with extensive polar ice caps.

About 40 million years ago, the ice sheet in Antarctica began, starting a new ice age. Over the last 3 million years, there have been cycles of glaciations with ice sheets advancing and retreating on 40,000-100,000-year time scales. The most recent of these ended about 10,000 years ago.

Oceanic Systems

Earth's surface is 71% water, most of which is found in the earth-encircling ocean. Seawater and ice make up 99.35% of all the water on Earth. The volume of the oceans is more than one billion cubic kilometers.

The terms sea and ocean both refer to saltwater bodies. A sea is smaller than an ocean. A sea or ocean can contain other seas. The Mediterranean Sea contains seven smaller seas. When the term "the seven seas" is used, it refers to the known world of the fifteenth century mapmakers. The seven seas they put on their maps were the Mediterranean Sea, the Red Sea, the East African Sea, the West African Sea, the China Sea, the Persian Gulf, and the Indian Ocean. Geographers today refer to five oceans: Pacific, Atlantic, Indian, Southern, and Arctic. However, there are only three ocean basins: the large Pacific, the Atlantic, and the small Indian. The water from all the oceans and seas interconnects and flows around and over the world.

World weather patterns are greatly influenced by ocean surface currents in the upper layer of the ocean. Surface currents are river-like bodies of water that do not extend very deeply under the surface of the ocean. These currents continuously move along the ocean surface in specific directions, usually long distances in huge curved paths.

Ocean currents that flow deep below the surface are called sub-surface currents. These currents are influenced by such factors as the location of landmasses in the current's path and the earth's rotation. These currents flow in opposite directions from surface currents and travel much more slowly. Deep currents are generated by differences in densities of ocean waters rather than by the wind.

Differences in water density can create ocean currents. Water found near the bottom of oceans is the coldest and the densest. Water tends to flow from a denser area to a less dense area. Currents that flow because of a difference in the density of the ocean water are called density currents. Water with a higher salinity is denser than water with a lower salinity. Water that has salinity different from the surrounding water may form a density current.

Surface currents are caused by winds and are classified by temperature. Cold currents originate in Polar regions and flow through surrounding water that is measurably warmer. Those currents with a higher temperature than the surrounding water are called warm currents and can be found near the equator. These currents follow swirling routes around the ocean basins and the equator. Ocean currents carry vast amounts of heat energy from the equator toward the poles.

The Gulf Stream and the California Current are the two main surface currents that flow along the coastlines of the United States. The Gulf Stream is a warm current in the Atlantic Ocean that carries warm water from the equator to the northern parts of the Atlantic Ocean. The Gulf Stream carries warm water north along the coast of the U.S.. As it moves north, it cools and becomes denser. Then it sinks into the deep sea near Greenland. When it sinks, it pulls more water northward to fill its place, creating a pattern of movement similar to a conveyor belt. The Gulf Stream was studied and named by Benjamin Franklin. The California Current is a cold current that originates in the Arctic regions and flows southward along the west coast of the United States.

The movement of an ocean current in one direction or another is influenced by the Coriolis effect. The Coriolis effect is due to the rotation of the earth. Ocean currents generated by winds move in a clockwise direction in the Northern Hemisphere and in a counterclockwise direction in the Southern Hemisphere.

The North Atlantic acts as a giant heat pump that cyclically warms and cools the atmosphere over the course of decades. The eastern part of the Atlantic Ocean is salty due to the emptying of the Mediterranean Sea which is shallow. The western part is relatively fresh. As the Gulf Stream pushes warm water into the North Atlantic a high-pressure region is created. The clockwise flow out of the region draws fresh water in from the west. The lighter (less salty) water does not sink easily so it slows the Gulf Stream. The northward flow of heat energy is reduced, so the water cools and starts sinking again. That creates a low-pressure zone which draws water in a counterclockwise direction, getting saltier water which is denser and sinks faster. One slow-down-speed-up cycle takes 40-60 years.

The movement of ocean water is caused by the wind, the sun's heat energy (convection), the earth's rotation, the moon's gravitational pull on earth, and underwater earthquakes. Most ocean waves are caused by the impact of winds. Wind blowing over the surface of the ocean transfers energy (friction) to the water and causes waves to form.

Waves are also formed by seismic activity on the ocean floor. A wave formed by an undersea volcanic eruption or earthquake is called a seismic sea wave, or a tsunami. These powerful waves can be very destructive, with wave heights of 30 meters or more near the shore. The crest of a wave is its highest point. The trough of a wave is its lowest point. The distance from wave top to wave top is the wavelength. The wave period is the time between the crests of two successive waves.

Waves "break" as they approach the shore and interact with the seafloor. The strength of the wind and the slope of the beach determine the shape of a breaking wave. (See Coasts for those descriptions.) The water particles in the wave move in a circular pattern that becomes more compressed and elliptical as it nears the shore. The particles slow in the trough but not in the crest, until eventually the crest overtakes the rest of the wave and spills over.

Extremely large waves are caused by the winds of hurricanes and other storms. The Beaufort Scale, which ranges from 0 to 12, is commonly used to quantify the strength of the wind. For example, a wind of 0 is a calm day. A wind of 6 is a strong breeze which produces waves of 3 meters in height (9-10 feet). Hurricane force winds are measured at 12 and produce 14-meter (50-ft) waves.

Ocean Basins

The primary component of the ocean floor is basalt. This is because oceanic crust primarily forms via mid-ocean ridges (or divergent ocean plate boundaries), where the spreading apart of two ocean plates results in high levels of volcanic activity. Magma will ooze out between the two diverging plates and cool into the basalt which composes much of the ocean floor. Because of this the ocean floor is very dense – around 3 g/cm3. This basalt layer is then covered over time with a thin layer of various other organic and inorganic sediments.

Since oceans lie lower than continents, they serve as basins that collect sediment eroded from the continents. Ocean basins also serve as resting places for the skeletons of carbonate- and silica-secreting organisms.

Ocean basins may be actively changing size or may be inactive, depending on whether there is a moving plate tectonic boundary associated with it. The elements of an active - and growing - oceanic basin include an elevated mid-ocean ridge and flanking abyssal hills leading down to abyssal plains. The elements of an active oceanic basin often include the oceanic trench associated with a subduction zone.

The ocean floor has many of the same features that are found on land. The ocean floor has higher mountains than those present on land, extensive plains and deeper canyons than those present on land. Oceanographers have named different parts of the ocean floor according to their structure. The major parts of the ocean floor are:

The **continental shelf** is the sloping part of the continent that is covered with water extending from the shoreline to the continental slope.

The **continental slope** is the steeply sloping area that connects the continental shelf and the deep-ocean floor.

The **continental rise** is the gently sloping surface at the base of the continental slope.

The **abyssal plains** are the flat, level parts of the ocean floor.

A **seamount** is an undersea volcano peak.

A **guyot** is a submerged flat-topped seamount.

Mid-ocean ridges are continuous undersea mountain chains that are found mostly in the middle portions of the oceans.

Ocean trenches are long, elongated narrow troughs or depressions formed where ocean floors collide with another section of ocean floor or continent. The deepest trench in the Pacific Ocean is the Marianas Trench which is about 11 km deep.

Ooze is the name given to the sediment that contains at least 30% plant or animal shell fragments. Ooze contains calcium carbonate. Deposits that form directly from sea water in the place where they are found are called authigenic deposits. For example, manganese nodules are authigenic deposits found over large areas of the ocean floor.

Although the age of the oceans is approximated at around 4 billion years, there are no rocks that can be found there that are older than around 180 million years. This is because the ocean floor is more quickly depleted and renewed. Because the ocean floor is compose of much denser materials than continental crust are, oceanic plates will subduct when they come into contact with other types of plates. New oceanic crust will then be formed at divergent oceanic boundaries, resulting in a sort of cycling process with the formation of the ocean floor.

Coasts

The shoreline is the boundary where land and sea meet. Shorelines mark the average position of sea level, which is the average height of the sea without consideration of tides and waves. Shorelines are classified according to the way they were formed. The three types of shorelines are: submerged, emergent, and neutral. When the sea has risen, or the land has sunk, a submerged shoreline is created. An emergent shoreline occurs when the sea falls or the land rises. A neutral shoreline does not show the features of a submerged or an emergent shoreline. A neutral shoreline is usually observed as a flat, broad beach.

A steep, rocky shore develops a number of features. Storm waves scour out a hollow or notch at the height of the wave. The notch is above average sea level and is easily seen after waves quiet down. A sea stack is an island of resistant rock left after weaker rock is worn away by waves and currents. Rock fragments broken from the cliff are ground up and used as scouring tools. As rock particles roll back and forth, they cut a smooth, flat surface just below sea level. This bench, or marine terrace, may be worn inland so far that water is too shallow for waves to erode any further. Thus, a sea cave is formed.

On low, gently sloping shores, waves only rearrange the shore sediment unless the shore is irregular. Erosion is important if headlands extend out from shore into deep water. If waves strike headlands at other than 90º, they are reflected. A current forms and water flows parallel to the shore. This longshore current carries loose sediment almost like a river of sand. If the shoreline bends, the material carried by the waves in a longshore current is deposited in open water and forms a sand bar. A spit is formed when a weak longshore current drops its load of sand as it turns into a bay. Therefore, a spit is really a sand bar that is connected to the curving shoreline.

When a break occurs in the wave front, the longshore current escapes seaward as a rip current. Rip currents are narrow currents that flow seaward at a right angle to the shoreline. These currents are very dangerous to swimmers.

Most beach sands are composed of grains of resistant material like quartz and orthoclase, but coral or basalt are found in some locations. Many beaches have rock fragments that are too large to be classified as sand. The type of material found on beaches varies according to its source. The color of the sand gives a clue to its origin. Atlantic coast beaches have white sand composed of quartz from the eastern U.S. Gulf of Mexico beaches vary from white to light tan depending upon the shells that have been pulverized to create them. Hawaiian Islands have black sand due to broken fragments of volcanic rocks.

In warmer parts of the oceans, coral reefs may form. A coral reef is a limestone rock structure built by live coral which is attached to a rock or another coral and builds a limestone shell around itself. When the coral dies, other corals build upon its shell. Because coral reefs slow waves down, the waves deposit sediments on the reef. When the sediments become thick and lie above sea level, tropical plants may grow on them.

Along some coasts tides scour deep, narrow channels. Tides race up through these narrow openings, eroding the channels even deeper. On irregular coastlines, tides may be very high.

When tides and storm waves move together toward shore, damage can be great. Waves pile up on shore when winds blow toward land. When these storm waves strike shore, they have tremendous force. When the water moves seaward, it carries great amounts of sediment with it.

Deserts and Wind

Winds are active erosional agents where the climate is arid or there is a lack of plants. Winds erode in two ways. Deflation is the removal of loose material from the ground surface. Particles carried by the wind consist of clay, silt, dust, and sand. The more fine the particles, the farther they are carried and the higher in the air they are carried. The faster the wind blows and the stronger the wind is, the more particles it can carry. Larger particles rise only a few centimeters, so they roll and bounce along the ground. That process slowly wears away exposed rock. Rock particles that are worn away by this abrasion are then carried away by the wind.

If the particles blowing in the wind are quartz, volcanic glass or basaltic grains, the abrade the land, acting like a sandblasting machine. Wind erosion forms wind caves in many desert regions by wearing away less-resistant material. Rocks that are subjected to sandblasting develop flat surfaces facing the wind. If the wind comes from different directions at different times of the year, two flat faces meeting in a sharp angle may result. Materials that are too heavy to be moved by the wind are called desert pavements or lag gravels. Their surfaces may be either polished or pitted by the sand grains.

The amount of wind erosion depends on the size of the particles being carried, the speed of the wind, the length of time the wind blows, and the resistance of the exposed rock. Wind erosion polishes pebbles and boulders. A windbreak is used to decrease wind erosion and aid in wind deposition. Windbreaks can be fences, trees, buses, or buildings. Without windbreaks large amounts of topsoil can be removed by the wind.

In desert areas and along shorelines, windblown sand forms deposits near rocks and bushes. As the wind blows over these deposits, it is slowed down, and more sand is deposited. The mounds of sand continue to grow, eventually forming sand dunes. Sand dunes vary in shape and size and are constantly changing shape and size – and moving. The side of the dune facing the way the wind comes from has a gentle slope which permits sand to be carried to the top or crest of the dune. When the sand is dropped at the crest, it slides steeply down the other side which is called the slipface.

Sand dunes move in the direction the wind blows. They may not appear to move, but over time they can move hundreds of meters or only a few centimeters. They are always being eroded on one side and being built on the other side. Moving sand dunes can cover buildings, farmland, and trees. If plants take root in sand dunes, they help to anchor them. Even without vegetation, slow-moving dunes can become cemented in their lowest layers.

Dunes take various shapes. Along the Gulf Coast, winds during the summer are usually from the southeast but during the winter they come from the north or northwest. Dunes formed by summer winds are rearranged by winter winds. Because of this, the dunes tend to be more round and symmetrical. Often, star-shaped dunes form where the wind direction changes. The most common shape is a half-moon shape called Barchan. Other shapes include Transverse (elongated S-shape), Parabolic, and Longitudinal.

Some very fine particles of sand and silt are not deposited in dunes. They may be deposited many kilometers from where they were picked up. If many layers of fine sand and silt are deposited in the same area, loess is formed. Loess is light in color, fertile and can be many meters thick. Significant loess deposits are found near the northern and central parts of the Mississippi River Valley, in northeast China, and in the Gobi desert.

If winds erode material away to a depth that allows water to be accessed, vegetation can grow. An oasis of trees, shrubs and grasses thrives, showing that deserts can be fertile. The trees and shrubs serve as a windbreak against further erosion. However, sand dunes can cover an oasis.

A desert is a region that receives less than 25 cm (10 in) of rain or other precipitation per year. Vegetation is exceedingly sparse. One third of the Earth's surface is desert. Sand covers only about 20% of the Earth's deserts. There are six forms of deserts:

- Mountain and basin deserts – shadowed by mountains which receive all the preciptiation
- Hamada deserts – comprised of plateau landforms
- Regs – consist of rock pavements
- Ergs – formed by sand seas
- Intermontane Basins – located at very high altitudes, usually cold
- Badlands – located at the margins of arid lands comprised of clay-rich soil

Deserts contain valuable mineral deposits which are now exposed by erosion. Artifacts and fossils are preserved for observation. Groundwater leaches ore minerals and redeposits them in zones near the water table. This process concentrates these minerals as ore that can be mined. The Great Basin Desert of the U.S. is the source of boron used in the manufacture of glass and enamel, as a water softener and agricultural chemical and in pharmaceuticals. Sodium nitrate for explosives and fertilizer comes from the Atacama Desert of South America. Many valuable minerals are located in arid lands: copper in the U.S., Chile, Peru, and Iran; iron ore in Australia; chromite in Turkey; and gold, silver and uranium in Australia and the U.S. Some of the more productive petroleum areas on Earth are found in arid and semiarid regions of Africa and the Mideast.

Geologic Time

Prior to geology becoming a science, estimates of the earth's age (and the times of various events in history) were based on biblical texts. Even though the Bible never states any "real" timeframes, the use of generations of families and their ages when various events occurred gave inferred aging. A major event used for telling time was the flood during Noah's life. It was considered to be universal.

Geologic time can be thought of in terms of relative time or absolute time. Relative time relates to whether one even came before or after another event, but does not try to place exact years on events. Absolute time in geology measures whether an event took place a few thousand years ago or 65 billion years ago. It tries to place events on a time scale. Precision and accuracy are very difficult in terms of geologic time.

The modern geologic time scale started with Abraham Gottlob Werner. He divided time into primary, transition, secondary, tertiary, and quaternary.

Relative Geologic Time

Geologic time throughout the 1700s and most of the 1800s was confined to dating strata of rocks in relation to each other. Relative-age dating is still important for sequencing layers of sedimentary rock and fossils.

One of the principles used by geologists in determining the relative ages of different rock layers is the law of superposition. Superposition is the principle that layers that are farther down were deposited first, and layers of rock that are higher up were deposited last. In other words, the oldest rocks are at the bottom. This principle is typically applied when considering sedimentary rocks, which form layer upon layer. Each layer covers up the layer before it, allowing geologists to study the relative time periods.

Another tool that can be used in the process of determining the relative ages of rock formations are unconformities. An unconformity signifies an age gap in deposited rocks. For example, if sediment was being deposited over time, then for some reason it stopped and erosion began to occur. This would result, once sediment began to be deposited again, in a time gap in the ages of rocks. There are three important types of unconformities: angular unconformities, nonconformities and disconformities. Angular unconformities tend to be the most visually apparent of the three. This occurs when, during the time gap in question, the lower layers of rock undergo some sort of activity that causes them to angle so that they are no longer horizontal. Because of this they will be at a different angle than newer layers which are deposited horizontally on top. A disconformity refers to a situation in which a time gap and erosion occur, but the older and newer layers are still parallel (the older layers remain horizontal). The disconformity would therefore lie between two layers of parallel sedimentary rock. Nonconformities are unique from angular unconformities and disconformities in that they deal with types of rock other than sedimentary. When a nonconformity occurs sedimentary rock is deposited on layers of metamorphic or igneous rock that has undergone erosion. A situation such as this would tend to indicate that there has been a major change in the environment to result in the change in methods of rock formation.

Another element that can be used in relative dating is fault lines. Formations will always be older that the faults lines that run through them (otherwise they wouldn't be there). If a formation has a fault line that runs through lower layers, but not higher layers, then the lower layers must have been deposited before the fault, and the higher layers afterwards. Therefore, the lower layers are older than the higher layers.

The Principle of Uniformitarianism states that the processes that act on the earth's surface today are the same as the processes (weathering, erosion, and deposition) that have acted on the earth's surface throughout the past. The Law of Superposition is used by scientists to determine the relative ages of rock layers and the fossils in them.

Specific fossils, each of which lived at a specific time and for a limited period of time, are used as representative of those time periods. These fossils are called index fossils. Because fossils actually record the slow but progressive development of life, scientists can use them to identify rocks of the same age throughout the world.

Field Relations

The effects of seasonal changes are helpful in telling time in the field. Annual variations occur in such things as growth rings of trees and erosion and deposition of sediment. Any deposit that reflects a yearly cycle is a varve. Some the most easily interpreted varves are associated with glaciers. In and near most ice fields, the seasons of melting and freezing are sharply marked, and there are abundant lakes and ponds in which deposits may be preserved. Large quantities of sediment are deposited in spring and summer during the melting of ice and snow. That creates a thick layer of sediment that is coarser. Little to no sedimentation occurs in fall and winter. However, very fine clay particles and some dead organic matter may settle to the bottom of a pond or lake and form a thin layer of finer, darker material. Thus, each varve consists of two gradational parts. With erosion, many years of varves may be clearly exposed.

Absolute Geologic Time

Until radiometric dating (such as carbon dating) techniques became available in the mid-1900s, actual dating of rocks or determining their age was impossible. All radioactive elements are subject to decay – alpha, beta, or gamma – of specific types, in specific ways, and at regular half-life intervals.

Rocks contain minerals which decay radioactively over long periods of time. A geologist can take samples and determine how much of the minerals have decayed to determine how long it has been since the formation cooled last (i.e., how long the specific formation has existed as it is). Radioactive decay occurs in half lives. In other words, it takes a certain amount of time for half of the material to decay, say 30 million years. So, after 30 million years only one-half of the original material would still be present. After a second 30 million years (so after 60 million years had passed) an addition half will have decayed, resulting in one-fourth of the original product remaining.

Originally carbon-dating was used; however the half-life of carbon was much too short to tell very much in relation to the time scale of geology if a specimen was older than 50,000 years. Uranium-238 decays to Lead-206 in a half-life of 4.5 billion years which is a better fit for geological time. Uranium-235 to Lead-207 takes 704 million years, Thorium-232 to Lead-208 takes 14.0 billion years, and Potassium-40 to Argon-40 takes 1.25 billion years. The Potassium-Argon method can be used on rocks as young as a few thousand years as well as on the oldest rocks known. When feasible, two or more methods of analysis are used on the same specimen to confirm results.

In the 1800s three geological eras were widely recognized: the Paleozoic, the Mesozoic, and the Cenozoic. They roughly coincided with Werner's Primary, Secondary and Tertiary. These became the eras. The subdivisions of these eras, the periods, became known by names that reflect the places where the rocks are particularly well exposed: Devonian for Devonshire, England or Permian for the Perm Basin in Russia. Some periods were named for ancient people groups such as Cambrian and Ordovician. And some bear names related to the character of rocks deposited during that time such as Carboniferous for rocks that have coal deposits. The periods have been further subdivided into epochs.

Eon	Era	Period	Epoch	Million Yrs
Phanerozoic	Cenozoic	Quaternary	Holocene	
			Pleistocene	1.5
		Neogene (Tertiary)	Pliocene	
			Miocene	23
		Paleogene (Tertiary)	Oligocene	
			Eocene	
			Paleocene	65
	Mesozoic	Cretaceous		146-65
		Jurassic		208-146
		Triassic		245-208
	Paleozoic	Permian		290-245
		Pennsylvanian		323-290
		Mississippian		363-323
		Devonian		409-363
		Silurian		439-409
		Ordovician		510-439
		Cambrian		570-510
Pre-Cambrian		Proterozoic		2500-570
		Archean		3800-2500
		Hadean		4600-3800

The Pre-Cambrian Eon shows no sign of life until the Proerozoic Period. Archean rocks are mostly metamorphic while Proterozoic rocks are sedimentary, igneous, and metamorphic. There is evidence of two major ice ages.

The Paleozoic Era had seven Periods. The earliest good fossils are from the Cambrian Period. These include invertebrates like trilobites and brachiopods. It is believed that there was widespread flooding of continents which produced limestones, shales, and sandstones. North America probably separated from Europe.

The water retreated for part of the Ordovician Period, but there may have been more shallow flooding later in the period as fossils reveal many shallow sea sediments. Fossils from this period include fish, amphibians and reptiles. North America and Europe moved slowly southward in close proximity to each other.

The Silurian Period had another ice age followed by more flooding and drying out. Limestone and mudstone from this period is prevalent. Fossils of the earliest plants are from the Silurian Period.

During the Devonian Period continents moved together to produce large continents with desert sandstones (Old Red Sandstone) and river deposits. In the United States, the Mississippian and Pennsylvanian Periods are distinct, but most of the world refers to those two periods as the Carboniferous Period. This was a time of much growth – especially plant growth - that died and was buried under layers of sediment, thus forming carboniferous coal. North America and Europe may have been near the equator and the southern hemisphere may have been covered in ice by the end of this period.

During the Permian Period, Asia collided with Europe which produced the Ural Mountains. Seas withdrew, giving time for deposition of desert sandstones called the New Red Sandstone.

The Mesozoic Era consisted of the Triassic Period, the Jurassic Period, and the Cretaceous Period. During this time, many more animals must have roamed the earth as there are many animal fossils. The Mesozoic Era is called the Age of Reptiles as that is when the dinosaurs roamed the earth. Volcanic activity produced vast quantities of plateau basalts, especially in Siberia and South Africa.

Giant mosses and tree ferns were the most common forms of plants during the Triassic and Jurassic Periods. Palmlike seed plants called cycads and cone-bearing plants, conifers, like pine, cedar, spruce, and cypress were common. The Jurassic Period was a time of continent separation. Shallow seas may have flowed over the edges of continents. Shales, clays, limestones and sandstones formed. Dinosaurs flourished in the swampy areas. Climates were much milder during the Cretaceous Period. Hardwood trees like oak, elm, maple, birch, and beech were plentiful. Few marine sediments are available from this time. Large areas of chalk were laid down.

Most of the history we know is from the Cenozoic Era. Most sediments from this time are still sands and muds that have not been turned to solid rock. Animal and plant life as we know it has developed. Vast basalt deposits formed ocean floors. Many of the mountains such as the Himalayas, Alps, and Andes were formed by continental collisions.

In the Quaternary part of the Cenozoic Era, the great ice ages or glaciers developed and receded. This left the features that are prominent in today's landscapes – lakes, hills, basins, and many rocks that seem to be in the wrong places.

Structural Geology

The Earth's crust is always moving and changing. Wherever the rocks of the crust can be seen, evidence of rock movement can be seen. Some movements like earthquakes are rapid and large. Some movements happen slowly and continuously.

Sedimentary rock beds are separated by surfaces called bedding planes which are usually horizontal when the rocks are first formed. Many of the ancient sedimentary rocks are arranged at various angles to the horizontal and often to each other. Some appear vertical or even upside down.

The force that produces rock movement is called stress. Rock reacts to stress by changing its shape or volume or both. These deformations are called strain. Rocks have three strain responses: elastic deformation, plastic deformation, and rupture. In elastic deformation, the substance returns to its original shape and volume when the stress is removed. The deformation is proportional to the stress. In plastic deformation the substance undergoes a continuous change of shape and does not recover its original volume or shape. Usually the deformation is elastic up to a critical point (yield point). A rock will rupture or break apart if the pressure or stress becomes too great or the rocks are too hard to respond in a plastic or elastic way.

When rocks are deformed out of their original shape, they assume new patterns referred to as structural features. These features are joints, folds, faults, and unconformities. To describe the position in space of the rocks making up such structural features, geologists use two special measurements: dip and strike. The dip is the acute angle that a tilted rock layer makes with an imaginary horizontal plane. The direction of strike is always at right angles to the direction of the dip. The strike is the orientation of a line formed by the intersection of the bed with the horizontal plane.

Magma often forces its way into layers of sedimentary rock. When it hardens, it forms an igneous intrusion. The igneous intrusion is younger than the rock through which it passes. Igneous rock that forms on the surface is called an igneous extrusion. Igneous extrusions are younger than the layers underneath them.

Joints

The most common structural feature of rocks exposed at the surface is a joint. This is simply a break in the rock material without any relative movement of the rock on either side. Joints may have any orientation but in any given rock mass, joints tend to occur in sets with the fractures somewhat parallel to each other.

Joints may be a result of compression, tension or shear stress. Compression is a squeezing together type of force in which rocks move both up and down due to the sideways (sometimes torsional) squeezing. (Think of squeezing a ball of clay in your hand and having some of it squirt out at the top and some squirt out at the bottom.) A pulling apart force produces tension. Tension joints form a regular pattern at right angles to the tension. Both compression and tension produce strain and change the volume of rocks. Shearing, on the other hand, changes the shape but not the volume of the rocks as one block of rock is pushed past another.

Faults

Faults are fractures in the earth's crust which have been created by either tension or compression forces transmitted through the crust. The rupture point is exceeded. These forces are produced by the movement of separate blocks of crust. Earthquakes occur along faults. Fault movement leads to mountain building and volcanoes.

Faults are categorized on the basis of the relative movement between the blocks on both sides of the fault plane. The movement can be horizontal, vertical or oblique.

If the fracture, or fault plane, dips at some angle from the vertical, the mass of rock above the fault plane is called the hanging wall and the one beneath it the foot wall. Faults may be described on the basis of the relative movement of the foot wall to the hanging wall.

A dip-slip fault occurs when the movement of the plates is vertical and opposite (one part goes up and the other goes down). The displacement is in the direction of the incli-nation, or dip, of the fault. Dip-slip faults are classified as normal faults when the rock above the fault plane moves down relative to the rock below.

A normal fault is one in which the hanging wall has moved downward in relation to the foot wall. Normal faults are the result of tension, or pulling apart.

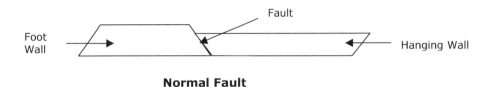

Normal Fault

Reverse faults are created when the hanging wall has moved upward relative to the foot rock below. Reverse faults are the result of compression. Reverse faults having a very low angle to the horizontal are also referred to as thrust faults.

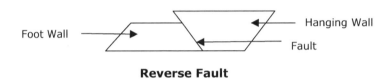

Reverse Fault

Faults in which the dominant displacement is horizontal movement along the trend or strike (length) of the fault are called strike-slip faults. These can be left lateral or right lateral. If you were walking along a road and had to jog to the right to get to the rest of the road, you would be witnessing a right lateral strike-slip fault. When a large strike-slip fault is associated with plate boundaries it is called a transform fault. The San Andreas Fault in California is a well-known transform fault.

Faults that have both vertical and horizontal movement are called oblique-slip faults.

When a block moves vertically downward between two faults, the structure is called a graben. If this forms a topographical feature on the surface, it is a rift valley. Death Valley in California is a rift valley. The valley of the Dead Sea in Israel and Jordan is an example of an active rift valley. The faults appear to be continuing their movement since the Jordan River deposits tons of sand and mud in the Dead Sea each year, but the Dead Sea never gets any shallower.

If a block is left upstanding as the rock masses at each side are downfaulted, the result is a horst. A geomorphological feature produced like this is called a block mountain.

Unconformities

In many places younger rocks are separated from older rocks by surfaces of erosion or of nondeposition. Such surfaces are called unconformities. They represent events in Earth history but events which are not preserved as rock material. Geologists recognize angular unconformities, disconformities, and nonconformities. In an angular unconformity there are two series of rock layers that meet in a sharp angle. With a disconformity, the two series of rock layers are parallel but there is an obvious line of erosion between them. And a nonconformity is an unconformity that develops when massive igneous rocks are exposed to erosion and then covered by sedimentary rock layers.

All three types of unconformities are found in the Grand Canyon. There is a nonconformity between the non–sedimentary basement schists and everything above. An angular unconformity lies between the downfaulted block of Precambrian sedimentary rock and the Cambrian sequence above it. A disconformity lies between the horizontal Cambrian and Devonian strata.

Folds

Crustal movements may press horizontal layers of sedimentary rock together from the sides, squeezing them into wavelike folds. Up-folded sections of rock are called anticlines (they have an "A" shape); down-folded sections of rock are called synclines ("U" shape). In an eroded anticline the oldest beds are in the center and in an eroded syncline the youngest beds will be seen in the center of the fold. Anticlines form ridges and hills while synclines form the valleys. The Appalachian Mountains (from Canada to Alabama) are an example of folded mountains with long ridges and valleys in a series of anticlines and synclines formed by folded rock layers.

Even though an anticline is an upward fold, it is not always higher than the surrounding land. The compression may not be great enough to bring the fold to the surface. Or the folds may be covered by new rock layers. Or the ridge may have eroded.

Interior of the Earth

The core, the center, of the earth is divided into the outer core and inner core. The density of the core is 10-12 grams per cubic centimeter which is considerable denser than iron at the surface of the earth at 2.5 grams per cubic centimeter. This is due to the increased pressure at the core. The inner core is thought to be a solid iron or solid iron-nickel. The earth's magnetic field is explained by understanding the iron core. The outer core is believed to be molten iron or a molten iron-nickel with some lighter elements like silicon, sulfur and oxygen.

The layer between the core and the crust is called the mantle. It is about 2900 km deep and is basically solid with some localized partial melting of the ferromagnesian silicates in the outermost layer. Below that are oxides and silicates of iron, magnesium, silicon and some minor elements which are all solids.

The lower mantle is the area from 2900 km to somewhere between 200 and 400 km below the earth's crust. Here there is a transition zone where earthquake wave velocities change. The change appears to be due to phase changes – changes in crystalline structure without changes in composition.

The boundary between the mantle and the crust is called the Mohorovicic discontinuity, or Moho. Just under this is the upper mantle which is made up of the lithosphere and asthenosphere. The lithosphere is a rigid layer that extends to a depth of about 100 kilometers. It contains the dozen or so massive plates upon which the continental and ocean basin crust ride as well as the crust itself. The asthenosphere is considered a low velocity zone because earthquake waves decrease in velocity as they move through it. This area is less rigid than the lithosphere. The upper mantle continues below the asthenosphere where it is very soft and partially molten.

Under the continents and oceans is the earth's crust which varies from 10 to 50 (sometimes considered 5-60 km) kilometers. Under oceans it is quite thin, but under continental mountains it becomes its thickest. However, the average density below oceans is 3 grams per cubic centimeter while it is only 2.2 grams per cubic centimeter under continents. The crust's density increases with increasing depth. This density difference occurs because of a difference in composition.

The earth's crust is composed almost entirely of different combinations of the eight most common elements: oxygen (46.6%), silicon (27.7%), aluminum (8.13%), iron (5.00%), calcium (3.63%), sodium (2.82%), potassium (2.59%), and magnesium (2.09%). Oceanic crust consists mainly of basaltic rocks rich in the heavier common metals like iron and magnesium. It is similar to the upper mantle. Continental crust is composed of a variety of rock types, but the predominant rocks are granites which are rich in silicates (silicon and oxygen).

All crust is recycled as a result of geological processes, but the average age of rock in continental crust is about 650 million years while oceanic crust is only about 60 million years. This difference is best explained by the theory of plate tectonics. Accordingly, oceanic crust appears to be recycled by subduction more frequently than continental crust.

Plate Tectonics

Data obtained from many sources led scientists to develop the theory of plate tectonics. This theory is the most current model that explains not only the movement of the continents, but also the changes in the earth's crust caused by internal forces. The basic concept for plate tectonics began with Alfred Wegener in the early 1900s. His theory of continental drift held that all continents were once one great continent which he called Pangaea. He felt that at some time, the continents began to break apart and float apart.

Evidences of plate tectonics include fossils, mountains, and glaciers. Fossils are preserved remains or evidence of plant or animal life. In most cases these evidences – bones, impressions, shells, leaves – were left in mud or sand and became a part of sedimentary rock. Fossils of the same animals and plants from the same time period have been found in rocks in countries that today are very far from each other – Australia, India, and South Africa.

The Cape Mountains of South Africa and the mountains near Buenos Aires, Argentina, are very similar folded mountains which in both cases end in the ocean. Not only is it very unusual for mountains to end in an ocean, but for two ranges that are so similar to end in the ocean makes them appear to have been connected at one time.

Glacier deposits found in South America, Africa, India, Australia, and Antarctica seem to match. The direction of flow of the glacier appears to have been the same on Africa and South America.

As scientists started studying the oceans in the late 1950s, the similarities to and differences from continents and other oceans became apparent. All oceans have mid-ocean ridges which form long chains of huge mountains. Rocks next to mid-ocean ridges are younger than those farther away, with the youngest rocks in the center of the ridges. Therefore, the idea of ocean floor spreading was born.

In today's theory the entire earth's lithosphere is broken into nine large sections, or plates, and several small ones. Plates are rigid blocks of earth's crust and upper mantle. The major plates are named after the continents they are "transporting."

The plates float on and move with a layer of hot, plastic-like rock in the upper mantle. Geologists believe that the heat currents circulating within the mantle cause this plastic zone of rock to slowly flow, carrying along the overlying crustal plates. In this way, the surface of the earth is in constant motion.

The major lithospheric plates are named for surface features found on them. The largest plate is the Pacific Plate which includes about one-fifth of the earth's surface. The other plates are the North American, South American, Eurasian, African, Australian, and Antarctic Plates. The North American includes North America but extends into the Atlantic Ocean as does the Eurasian. There are also several smaller plates. For example, the Arabian plate includes the Arabian peninsula, the Red Sea, and the Persian Gulf. The Pacific plate is the only one that does not contain any continental crust.

One of the many unique features of the Earth which make it difficult for astronomer's to determine whether or not any other planet is capable of sustaining life to the extent that the earth is the presence of tectonic plates. The tectonic plates are important for a number of reasons, such as the fact that they allow the earth to maintain a stable internal temperature and are responsible for the magnetic poles (which help protect against solar flares). Although it is not sure whether tectonic plates are truly essential in the development of life, they do give the Earth many unique properties. So far, no other planets have been discovered to have active tectonic plates (although there is some evidence that Mars may have once had them in its early history).

Plate Movements

The movement of the plates may be related to convection currents within the earth. A convection current is the movement of gases or liquids caused by differences in temperatures. Major plate separation lines lie along the ocean floors. Molten rock rises, separating (diverging) the plates, continuously forming new ocean crust and creating new and taller mountain ridges under the ocean. The Mid-Atlantic is one of the major areas of divergence. Currents of hot mantle rock rise and separate at this point of divergence, creating new oceanic crust at the rate of 2 to 10 centimeters per year. The Mid-Atlantic Range which runs north to south through the Atlantic Ocean basin divides it into two nearly equal parts and shows evidence from mapping of such deep-ocean floor changes.

Movement of these crustal plates creates areas where the plates converge as well as areas where the plates diverge. Convergence is when the oceanic crust collides with either another oceanic plate or a continental plate. The oceanic crust sinks forming an enormous trench known as a subduction zone and generating volcanic activity. Portions of the lithosphere are dragged into the mantle. Then some of this material melts and volcanoes erupt. In time, a series of volcanic islands such as the Aleutian Islands is formed parallel to the trench.

Convergence also includes continent to continent plate collisions. When two plates slide past one another a transform fault is created. These movements produce many major features of the earth's surface, such as mountain ranges, volcanoes, and earthquake zones. Most of these features are located at plate boundaries, where the plates interact by spreading apart, pressing together, or sliding past each other. These movements are very slow, averaging only a few centimeters a year. The crustal movement which is identified by plates sliding sideways past each other produces a plate boundary characterized by major faults that are capable of unleashing powerful earthquakes. The San Andreas Fault forms such a boundary between the Pacific Plate and the North American Plate.

When two plates are sliding past each other, rather than pushing into each other or pulling apart from each other, the result is a transform plate boundary, or a transform fault. Transform faults are most commonly found in the ocean, but one very prominent example is the San Andreas Fault in California. The only real result of a transform fault is a large number of earthquakes and the plates move. Transform faults are nearly always connected at the ends with other types of plate boundaries. For example, a transform fault may occur as a mid-oceanic ridge pushes the crust material it produces past other sections of the ocean floor which are not part of the ridge.

When two tectonic plates collide, a possible result is subduction. Subduction refers to situations in which one of the plates is pushed beneath the other. This occurs in the case of ocean-ocean and ocean-continent collisions. When subduction occurs it results in a number of occurrences. For example, as the plate is pushed down into the mantle it will result in increased volcanic activity about the subducted plate. Therefore, volcanic activity along a plate boundary is a sign of subduction. Another result of subduction is numerous earthquakes, and the emergence of mountain ranges (as one plate is subducted it will also push up on the plate above it, causing mountains). Trenches are another common feature of subduction zones.

Plate Boundaries

Boundaries form between spreading plates where the crust is forced apart in a process called rifting. Rifting occurs at mid-ocean ridges when lava erupts from a valley or rift that runs the length of the ridge. Rifting can also take place within a continent, splitting the continent into smaller landmasses that drift away from each other, thereby forming an ocean basin between them. The Red Sea is a product of rifting. As the ocean floor spreading takes place, lava cools and hardens to form rock which is added to the edges of the separating plates. In this way the plates are pushed apart and grow larger, and the ocean basin widens. This is the process that broke up the super continent Pangaea and created the Atlantic Ocean.

Even though the ocean floors are spreading, the earth is not getting any larger. Older rocks of the ocean floor get pushed deep into the earth along trenches which are long V-shaped valleys. This often happens at boundaries between plates, near the edges of oceans. When a plate of ocean crust collides with a plate of continental crust, the more dense oceanic plate slides under the lighter continental plate and plunges into the mantle. This process is called subduction, and the site where it takes place is called a subduction zone. There is a balance (a type of equilibrium) between the building of new plate material at the ocean ridges and the destroying of old plate material at the trenches.

At plate boundaries where two oceanic crusts are diverging a phenomenon occurs which is known as sea floor spreading. As the plates pull apart, volcanic activity occurs and basalt pushes up through the diverging plates to form new ocean crust. This means that the youngest rocks will be located near the actual plate boundary and older rocks will radiate out parallel to it in either direction (the oldest rocks, therefore, would be nearest to continents). The most well-known divergent ocean boundary is the Mid-Atlantic Ridge in the middle of the Atlantic Ocean. Determining the rate of sea floor spreading requires knowledge of the distance between two points, and the difference in their ages.

For example, a point on the ocean floor is 2 kilometers from the plate boundary is dated to be 10,000 years old. In this example, the two points would be the plate boundary, corresponding to distance zero and age zero for the sake of simplicity, and the known point. Because the movement happens so slowly the measurements are usually converted to centimeters, and then the rate of seafloor spreading would be found by dividing distance by time. The resulting calculation would be 200,000cm/10,000yrs=20 cm/yr.

It is at plate boundaries that the majority of volcanoes and earthquakes take place. Faults and earthquakes go hand-in-hand just as volcanoes and mountain-building are related.

While the result of divergent ocean-ocean boundaries is sea floor spreading, when two ocean plates collide the result is much different. At a convergent ocean-ocean boundary, whichever of the ocean plates is older (and correspondingly more dense) will subduct, and be pushed underneath the other. This will result in volcanic activity above the subducted plate, and the result will be the formation of an island arc. It is important to distinguish island arcs from island chains. Island chains are straight and form over hot spots in the mantle. Although island arcs consist of a chain of islands, the chain is curved and they form at convergent ocean-ocean boundaries. Examples of island arcs include Japan and the Aleutian Islands.

Mechanisms of Producing Mountains

Mountains are a dominant landscape feature of the continents. They often occur in long chains, following somewhat curved lines that are concentrated toward the margins of the continents. The central areas of continents seem relatively devoid of mountains at this time. However, there may have been interior mountains that have basically disappeared due to glaciers and erosion. Orogeny is the term given to natural mountain building.

Mountains are not restricted to continents. Many mountains in the ocean basins are much taller than those on the continents. For example, the Mid-Atlantic Ridge roughly parallels the outlines of the continents and is nearly midway between them. It stands as much as 6,000 feet above the ocean bottom and is covered in places by 9,000 feet of water. In a few places its peaks protrude above the water to form islands such as the Azores, St. Helena, and Tristan da Cunha. Similar ridges characterize other oceans.

A mountain is terrain that has been raised high above the surrounding landscape by volcanic action or some form of tectonic plate collisions. The plate collisions could have been intercontinental or ocean floor collisions with a continental crust (subduction). The physical composition of mountains can include igneous, metamorphic, and/or sedimentary rocks; some may have rock layers that are tilted or distorted by plate collision forces.

There are many different types of mountains. The physical attributes of a mountain range depends upon the angle at which plate movement thrust layers of rock to the surface. Many mountains (Adirondacks, Southern Rockies) were formed along high angle faults.

Folded mountains (Alps, Himalayas) are produced by the folding of rock layers during their formation. The Himalayas are the highest mountains in the world and contain Mount Everest which rises almost 9 km above sea level. The Himalayas were formed when India collided with Asia. The movement which created this collision is still in process at the rate of a few centimeters per year.

Plateaus often form next to folded mountains. A plateau is made of layers of flat-lying rocks that are high above sea level. They are raised by the same forces that caused the folding and faulting – compression and tension –but are not themselves folded. The Appalachian plateau and the Colorado plateau were formed in this way.

Plateaus can also be formed by lava flows. Lava can reach the surface of the earth through large cracks. As the lava cools, layers of rock are formed. The lava shrinks to form joints with a distinct six-sided pattern called columnar jointing which can be seen along the sides of the plateau where a river has cut through it. Examples of lava plateaus include the Columbia plateau in Oregon, Washington, and Idaho; the Deccan plateau in India; the Ethiopian plateau in Africa; and the large plateau in southern Brazil.

Fault-block mountains (Utah, Arizona, and New Mexico) are created when plate movement produces tension forces instead of compression forces. The area under tension produces normal faults and rock along these faults is displaced upward.

Dome mountains are formed as magma tries to push up through the crust but fails to break the surface. Dome mountains resemble a huge blister on the earth's surface. Upwarped mountains (Black Hills of South Dakota) are created in association with a broad arching of the crust.

Volcanism is the term given to the movement of magma through the crust and its emergence as lava onto the earth's surface. Volcanic mountains are built up by successive deposits of volcanic materials.

An active volcano is one that is presently erupting or building to an eruption. A dormant volcano is one that is between eruptions but still shows signs of internal activity that might lead to an eruption in the future. An extinct volcano is said to be no longer capable of erupting. Most of the world's active volcanoes are found along the rim of the Pacific Ocean (the edge of the Pacific Plate), which is also a major earthquake zone. This curving belt of active faults and volcanoes is often called the Ring of Fire.

The world's best known volcanic mountains include: Mount Etna in Italy and Mount Kilimanjaro in Africa. The Hawaiian Islands are actually the tops of a chain of volcanic mountains that rise from the ocean floor. There are three types of volcanic mountains: shield volcanoes, cinder cones and composite volcanoes.

Shield Volcanoes are associated with quiet eruptions. Lava emerges from the vent or opening in the crater and flows freely out over the earth's surface until it cools and hardens into a layer of igneous rock. A repeated lava flow builds this type of volcano into the largest volcanic mountain. Mauna Loa found in Hawaii, is the largest volcano on earth.

Cinder Cone Volcanoes are associated with explosive eruptions as lava is hurled high into the air in a spray of droplets of various sizes. These droplets cool and harden into cinders and particles of ash before falling to the ground. The ash and cinder pile up around the vent to form a steep, cone-shaped hill called the cinder cone. Cinder cone volcanoes are relatively small but may form quite rapidly.

Composite Volcanoes are described as being built by both lava flows and layers of ash and cinders. Mount Fuji in Japan, Mount St. Helens in Washington, USA and Mount Vesuvius in Italy are all famous composite volcanoes.

Gravity and Isostasy

The principle of isostasy suggests that if gravity were the only force acting on the earth's surface, all masses of surface rock would be standing at heights determined by their thickness and the ratio of their specific gravity to that of the rocks supporting them. The expectation would be that if materials are removed from a mountain by erosion, the land will rise to compensate. Therefore, as a mountain range is eroded, the reduced range would rebound upwards to a certain extent to be eroded further. Some of the rock strata now visible at the ground surface may have spent much of their history at great depths below the surface buried under other strata.

When continents collide, the continental crust may thicken at their edges in the collision. If this happens, much of the thickened crust may move downwards rather than up as with the iceberg analogy. The idea of continental collisions building mountains "up" is, therefore, a simplification. Instead, the crust thickens and the upper part of the thickened crust may become a mountain range. However, some continental collisions are far more complex than this, and the region may not be in isostatic equilibrium. Geophysics - Earthquakes and Seismology

There are hundreds of thousands of earthquakes around the world each year. In any 24-hour period there are over 400 earthquakes worldwide. Most are not noticed or felt by humans or animals but detected only by sensitive instruments. (However, it is important to note that animals feel many minor earthquakes that people do not. Animals that are not chained or fenced will know to flee an area just prior to an earthquake or tsunami.) Although earthquakes can occur anywhere, they are concentrated in areas of tectonic activity like the boundaries of plates.

The majority of earthquakes occur in belts or zones surrounding stable areas. The most active zone is the entire border of the Pacific Ocean which accounts for 80% of all earthquakes. Japan, western Mexico, Melanesia, and the Philippines have a high proportion of quake activity. The Mediterranean and Trans-Asiatic zone accounts for 15% of earthquake activity.

Studying earthquakes and seismic waves gave geologists a broader knowledge of the Earth's interior. Earthquakes occur when the ground is displaced, or faulted, because of a sudden release of built-up stress. Stress can build up, for instance, when parts of the crust are moving in different directions and become temporarily stuck because of friction. When the stress becomes too great, the rocks tear apart and snap back into unstrained positions in a process known as elastic rebound.

As the rocks begin to reach such a rupture point, small shocks called foreshocks are sometimes felt – they may be referred to as mini-earthquakes. When an earthquake occurs, energy is released in the form of seismic waves that travel away from the focus, or origin, of the quake. The point on the earth's surface that is directly above the earthquake's focus (source) is called the epicenter. Minor adjustments that occur after the break are called aftershocks.

Seismic waves are classified as surface waves – which travel through the crust only – and body waves – which penetrate deeply into the earth. Most of the damage of earthquakes is caused by seismic surface waves. These surface waves are like ripples when a stone is thrown into water. They cause rocks and soil to move in a series of ripples. Surface waves travel from the area directly above the focus (epicenter) out along the crust's surface to a recording station.

One of two types of body waves, the Primary or P Waves, move through the Earth at 5 to 15 kilometers per second. The other type of body waves, the Secondary or S Waves, move much more slowly. The difference in these two times is measured by a seismograph. The P Wave is a compressional wave like a sound wave. It travels in the same direction as its originating force and alternately compresses and expands the rock, water, and air through which it travels. The S Wave is a transverse or shear wave. Its energy travels side to side. It moves perpendicular to its source and can only travel through solids (not water or air).

The P Waves and S Waves travel from the focus of an earthquake through the interior of the earth to a recording station. The denser the solid, the faster the P Waves and S Waves move. The waves bend when they cross boundaries between materials of different densities. Since the P Waves travel faster than the S Waves, they arrive at the recording station first.

Earthquakes are described according to their magnitude and intensity. The Richter Scale measures the magnitude, or amount of earth shaking, of the earthquake. Since it is based on a logarithmic scale, a magnitude of 6 is ten times as strong (10 times as much shaking and displacement) as a magnitude of 5 and 100 times as strong as one of 4. Any earthquake of a magnitude greater than 2.0 is considered a major earthquake. There is no upper limit, but the greatest earthquake that has been recorded was just under 10.0.

An undersea megathrust earthquake of magnitude 9.0 struck off the western coast of Sumatra, Indonesia on December 26, 2004. The earthquake was the strongest in the world since the 9.2-magnitude Good Friday Earthquake which struck Alaska, USA in

1964, and the fourth largest since 1900. More than 140,000 deaths were caused by resulting tsunami, which in Thailand were up to 10 meters (33 feet) tall, and struck within three hours of the initial event.

Multiple tsunamis struck and ravaged coastal regions all over the Indian Ocean, devastating many regions including various Indonesian provinces, the coast of Sri Lanka, coastal areas of India, islands off of Thailand, and even as far away as Somalia which is 4,100 km (2,500 mi) west of the epicenter.

The Richter Scale does not measure the amount of damage done. The amount of damage done depends on the magnitude of the earthquake, the composition and structure of the underlying rock through which the earthquake travels, the proximity and structures of buildings, and the proximity of people to the earthquake's epicenter.
The Modified Mercalli scale uses Roman numerals to indicate an earthquake's effects on people and structures. The scale goes from I to XII. On the scale, XI indicates a quake that causes nearly total damage. That would mean that rivers are deflected, landslides occur, huge rock masses are shifted, and cities are reduced to rubble.
Earthquakes can inflict major damage on an area, but the after-effects are even worse. Fire is one of the greatest hazards after an earthquake. It can cause as much as 95% of all the damage. The earthquake can cause chemical spills and all types of utility (electricity and gas) line breaks which lead to fires. It breaks communication lines and topples towers used by cell phones. It can also rupture water lines and cause roads to be completely blocked which keeps the fires from being extinguished.

Seismic sea waves (tsunami) are especially damaging and dangerous. If the earthquake is underwater, the tsunami can strike without warning. The impending approach of a tsunami is heralded by a quiet withdrawal of the sea from the shore line with a speed and to a distance that exceeds any low tide. Then the water returns in a great surging sweep, piling higher and higher as it approaches the shore. It can easily become a wall of water from 10 to 30 meters high.

The results of an earthquake can be seen in cracks in the ground, landslides, faulting, and various changes in land levels. Buildings anchored in sand, gravel or clay sustain far more damage than those on bedrock.

Earthquake prediction is becoming more accurate and reliable as many more recording stations all over the world have become active. Some of the things that predict an impending earthquake include: changes in the speeds of primary and secondary waves, slight changes in the tilt of the earth's surface, slight rising or sinking of land near a fault, and changes in water levels in wells.

Geomagnetics

The earth has magnetic poles located about 1920 kilometers from the geographical North and South Poles of the Earth. They change slightly in position every year. The magnetic field of the earth is referred to as the magnetosphere. It extends beyond the atmosphere more than 64,000 kilometers into space. The exact origin of the magnetic field is unknown, but could be due to the dense iron core of the earth or a combination of the earth's rotation and currents caused by temperature differences within the earth.

Some scientists believe that the magnetic poles have reversed at times in the Earth's history – the north magnetic pole has become the south magnetic pole and the south magnetic pole has become the north magnetic pole. This may have occurred several times.

Magnetic particles in rocks formed at a particular time will align to show the current polarity at the time they were formed. The ocean floor is divided into stripes, each stripe magnetized in a different direction. The pattern of magnetization at one side of the ridge is a mirror image of that on the other side of the ridge. This seems to confirm sea floor spreading and changing magnetic poles.

The geographical North Pole forms an axis with the geographical South Pole. The Earth "turns on its axis." Magnetic lines of force extend between the magnetic north pole and the magnetic south pole.

The use of satellites led to the discovery of the presence of atmospheric zones of highly charged particles. These particles are trapped within the earth's magnetic field about 2,400 to 19,000 kilometers from the surface of the Earth. There are at least two regions, or belts, of radiation surrounding the earth, now known as the Van Allen Radiation Belts. The inner belt contains many protons (positively charged particles) while the outer belt contains many electrons (negatively charged particles). The Van Allen Radiation Belts show the invisible magnetic lines of force around the earth like iron filings show the magnetic lines of force around a magnet.

Minerals and Energy Resources

Nearly everything in our world starts with something that is either grown or mined as those are the main two sources of raw materials. Some of the things used in daily life that contain minerals are paper, walls of buildings, photographs, pens and pencils, cans and bottles of soda, telephones, televisions, and computers. The U.S. Bureau of Mines calculates that an average American will use almost 1 million kilograms of minerals and metals in his or her lifetime. That includes over 500,000 kg of sand and gravel, 40,000 kg of iron and steel, 12,000 kg of clay, 11,800 kg of salt, 360 kg of lead, almost 13,000 kg of phosphate and potash, 1400 kg of aluminum, 680 kg of copper, and 380 kg of zinc.

Non-living renewable resources include water, air, and soil. Water is renewed in a natural cycle called the water or hydrologic cycle. Air is a mixture of gases. Oxygen is given off by plants and taken in by animals that in turn expel the carbon dioxide that the plants need. Soil is another renewable resource. Fertile soil is rich in minerals. When plants grow they remove the minerals and make the soil less fertile. However, as plants die and are recycled as part of the soil, they replenish and fertilize the soil.

Nonrenewable resources are not easily replaced in a timely fashion. Minerals are nonrenewable resources. Quartz, mica, salt, sulfur, and coal are some examples. Mining depletes these resources so society may benefit. Glass is made from quartz, electronic equipment from mica, and salt has many uses. Sulfur is used in medicine, fertilizers, paper, and matches. Coal is used to generate electricity.

Limestone and granite are used in building. Iron is used in the making of steel. Gypsum is important for making drywall. Sand and gravel are used in huge amounts for the cement of roads and buildings.

Metals are among the most widely used nonrenewable resource. Metals must be separated from the ore. Iron is our most important ore. Gold, silver and copper are often found in a more pure form called native metals.

Environmental Geography

As water moves through wetlands (marshes and swamps) matter suspended in the water is trapped by plant roots or settles out as sediment. Marshes and swamps provide a service to humans and animals by filtering and cleaning polluted water. They also provide a home to a great variety of wildlife. The past century has seen the loss of huge amounts of wetlands worldwide to "provide" for projects such as farming, housing, grazing, industry, and even parkland.

The most important agent of geological erosion is homo sapiens – us. Building dams, bridges, roads, and other parts of civilization seems to require the blasting of mountainsides. Rock and ore quarries are huge holes in the ground. Strip mines for coal and ore remove huge amounts of rock and soil. Forests are cleared and rocks are moved to provide for farming and grazing. By removing these upper layers of humus, roots, and grasses, the next layers are more easily washed or blown away and leave areas barren and untillable.

Even attempts to irrigate dry land can sometimes cause more problems than are solved. For example, when rivers flowing into the Aral Sea were diverted for irrigation, the Aral Sea began to dry up and the exposed salt was blown over the land which made it unfit for cultivation.

Coastal land can be easily affected by the attempts of man. If breakwaters are built (to protect harbors), they cause sandbars to form in unexpected places and even contribute to the harbor not being deep enough to be a harbor after a while. If sand and gravel are removed from a beach area, the pattern of coastal currents is changed. This can affect nearby villages in many ways – by causing the currents to wash the land out from beneath the village, by taking fish to a different area (removal of food or their form of making a living), or by washing other things into the village.

"Acid rain" is a broad term referring to a mixture of wet and dry deposition (deposited material) from the atmosphere containing higher than normal amounts of nitric and sulfuric acids. The precursors, or chemical forerunners, of acid rain formation result from both natural sources, such as volcanoes and decaying vegetation, and man-made sources, primarily emissions of sulfur dioxide (SO_2) and nitrogen oxides (NOx) resulting from fossil fuel combustion. In the United States, roughly 2/3 of all SO_2 and 1/4 of all NOx come from electric power generation that relies on burning fossil fuels, like coal. Acid rain occurs when these gases react in the atmosphere with water, oxygen, and other chemicals to form various acidic compounds. The result is a mild solution of sulfuric acid and nitric acid. When sulfur dioxide and nitrogen oxides are released from power plants and other sources, prevailing winds blow these compounds across state and national borders, sometimes over hundreds of miles.

As this acidic water flows over and through the ground, it affects a variety of plants and animals. In areas where the weather is dry, the acid chemicals may become incorporated into dust or smoke and fall to the ground through dry deposition, sticking to the ground, buildings, homes, cars, and trees. Dry deposited gases and particles can be washed from these surfaces by rainstorms, leading to increased runoff. This runoff water makes the resulting mixture more acidic. About half of the acidity in the atmosphere falls back to earth through dry deposition.

Acid rain causes acidification of lakes and streams and contributes to the damage of trees at high elevations (for example, red spruce trees above 2,000 feet) and many sensitive forest soils. In addition, acid rain accelerates the decay of building materials and paints as well as irreplaceable buildings, statues, and sculptures that are part of a nation's cultural heritage. Prior to falling to the earth, sulfur dioxide (SO_2) and nitrogen oxide (NOx) gases and their particulate matter derivatives—sulfates and nitrates—contribute to visibility degradation and harm public health.

Carbon dioxide, water vapor, and other gases pumped into the atmosphere as a side effect of industry change the balance of atmospheric gases and produce the greenhouse effect. The greenhouse effect takes place when the heat from the sun can pass through to the Earth's surface but the re-radiated heat finds it difficult to escape. As a result, the climate begins to warm more and more each year.

Studies have shown that freon, a propellant in aerosol sprays prior to 1978, was destroying the ozone layer and allowing too much ultraviolet light to reach the earth. When this happens, people get skin cancer more easily, crops are damaged, and changes take place in the weather and climate. Newer propellants such as nitrogen oxides and bromofluorocarbons may also damage the ozone layer or speed the greenhouse effect.

Every day tons of industrial wastes are produced. Many of these wastes are highly toxic. They can cause cancer, skin rashes, respiratory problems, and death. Some emit toxic fumes, others are toxic to the touch, and still others combine with elements in the soil or water to create toxic substances which can harm water that is used for drinking water or soil used for growing food for people or animals. Disposal methods for these wastes has become a huge problem. Nearly every method has drawbacks and opponents as well as advantages and proponents.

🎓 *Sample Test Questions*

1) The ability of a mineral to resist scratching is called

    A) Luster
    B) Durability
    C) Hardness
    D) Streak

The correct answer is C:) Hardness. The Mohs Scale of hardness identifies which minerals can scratch which other minerals and which ones resist scratching based on their degree of hardness.

2) The breaking of a mineral along definite planes is called

    A) Cleavage
    B) Fracture
    C) Crystalline lattice
    D) Crystal faces

The correct answer is A:) Cleavage. Cleavage occurs when a mineral breaks along definite planes while fracture occurs when a mineral breaks along an irregular (rough or jagged) surface.

3) The two most abundant elements in the earth's crust are

    A) Oxygen and silicon
    B) Oxygen and aluminum
    C) Silicon and aluminum
    D) Oxygen and carbon

The correct answer is A:) Oxygen and silicon. Oxygen makes up 46.6% and silicon makes up 27.7% of the earth's crust.

4) Which of the following internal crystalline structure of minerals does not have three axes at right angles to one another?

    A) Cubic
    B) Tetragonal
    C) Monoclinic
    D) Orthorhombic

The correct answer is C:) Monoclinic. Cubic has three axes at right angles and all of the same length; tetragonal has three axes at right angles with two of the same length; and orthorhombic has three axes at right angles with all three being different lengths. Monoclinic has three axes but one is not at right angles to the others and all three are of different lengths.

5) Ore minerals contain

    A) Iron or magnesium
    B) A useful metal or nonmetal that is easily extracted
    C) Oxides combined with a metal
    D) Feldspars of the continental crust

The correct answer is B:) A useful metal or nonmetal that is easily extracted. The ore must have a use and its extraction must be cost-effective.

6) The two most important identifying characteristics of a mineral are

    A) Cleavage and color
    B) Color and crystalline structure
    C) Crystalline structure and composition
    D) Composition and hardness

The correct answer is C:) Crystalline structure and composition. Although color, hardness, luster, specific gravity, solubility, cleavage, and magnetism can be aids in identifying a mineral, the two most important and distinguishing characteristics are composition and crystalline structure.

7) All of the following are igneous rocks EXCEPT

    A) Gneiss
    B) Granite
    C) Basalt
    D) Rhyolite

The correct answer is A:) Gneiss. Gneiss is a metamorphic rock, granite is a coarse-grained igneous rock, basalt is a fine-grained igneous rock, and rhyolite is an igneous rock that is a product of volcanoes.

8) Obsidian, also known as volcanic glass, was formed

    A) By magma that cooled under varying conditions
    B) By very slow cooling magma
    C) By magma that cooled in contact with other rock
    D) By very fast cooling magma

The correct answer is D:) By very fast cooling magma. Glassy texture means the magma cooled very fast and did not form crystals.

9) The largest type of igneous rock formation is a

    A) Laccolith
    B) Batholith
    C) Dike
    D) Stock

The correct answer is B:) Batholith. An igneous rock formation that has an exposed surface area of more than 100 square kilometers is called a batholith.

10) The lava from a volcano will produce

    A) Intrusive igneous rocks
    B) Extrusive igneous rocks
    C) Nonclastic sedimentary rocks
    D) Large-crystalled rocks

The correct answer is B:) Extrusive igneous rocks. Volcano flows produce small-crystalled extrusive igneous rocks such as basalt, andesite, rhyolite, felsites, obsidian, pumice and tuff.

11) The Ring of Fire describes a band of volcanoes that surround the

    A) Atlantic Ocean
    B) Indian Ocean
    C) Mediterranean Ocean
    D) Pacific Ocean

The correct answer is D:) Pacific Ocean. The Ring of Fire circumscribes the Pacific Ocean. There is also a string of volcanoes around the Mediterranean Ocean, but it is not called the Ring of Fire.

12) Volcanoes come in all of the following shapes EXCEPT

    A) Composite cone
    B) Shield volcano
    C) Caldera cone
    D) Basaltic flow

The correct answer is C:) Caldera cone. A caldera is formed by the collapse of the top of a volcano.

13) The most abundant sedimentary rocks are

    A) Limestone, sandstone, and shale
    B) Quartz, brick, and sandstone
    C) Mud, sand, and gravel
    D) Siltstone, sandstone, and limestone

The correct answer is A:) Limestone, sandstone, and shale. Shale accounts for over half of all sedimentary rock and together with limestone and sandstone accounts for 99% of all sedimentary rock.

14) The principal means of transporting sediments is

    A) Wind
    B) Water
    C) Gravity
    D) Storms

The correct answer is B:) Water. Water – in streams and glaciers, underground, and in ocean currents – is the principal means of transporting material from one place to another.

15) The clastic rocks in order from smallest to largest fragments would be

    A) Shale, conglomerate, sandstone
    B) Shale, sandstone, conglomerate
    C) Sandstone, shale, conglomerate
    D) Sandstone, conglomerate, shale

The correct answer is B:) Shale, sandstone, conglomerate. Shale particles are less than 0.004 mm, sandstone particles are 0.004 mm to 2.0 mm, and conglomerate particles are greater than 2.0 mm.

16) The processes by which sediments are transformed into solid sedimentary rocks is

    A) Cementation
    B) Compaction
    C) Precipitation
    D) Lithification

The correct answer is D:) Lithification. Lithification is the series of steps or processes of converting unconsolidated rock-forming materials such as sand, rocky fragments, and fossils into consolidated, coherent sedimentary rock. It includes compaction, desiccation (evaporation of water), cementation by precipitation, and recrystallization.

17) Evaporites include all EXCEPT

    A) Limestone
    B) Rock salt
    C) Anhydrite
    D) Gypsum

The correct answer is A:) Limestone. Rock salt, gypsum, and anhydrite are evaporites.

18) The fact that fossils of organisms that lived in shallow water can be found in horizontal sedimentary rock layers at great ocean depths probably means

    A) The cold water deep in the ocean kills shallow water organisms
    B) Sunlight once penetrated to the deepest parts of the ocean
    C) Organisms that live in deep water evolved from species that once lived in shallow waters
    D) Sections of the Earth's crust have changed their elevations relative to sea level

The correct answer is A:) The cold water deep in the ocean kills shallow water organisms. The shallow water organisms may have lived there when the ocean was shallow and the ocean has become deeper and deeper over the centuries, causing the water to get deeper and colder which would explain the death and burial of the organisms. Alternately, the shallow water organisms could have been washed into the deep water during a major storm such as a hurricane.

19) Metamorphic rock is frequently found

    A) On mountaintops that have horizontal layers containing marine fossils
    B) Along the interface of igneous intrusions and sedimentary bedrock
    C) Within a large lava flow
    D) As thin surface layers covering huge areas of the continents

The correct answer is B:) Along the interface of igneous intrusions and sedimentary bedrock. Metamorphic rocks surround a mountain core of magma for hundreds of kilometers. Metamorphism occurs near the contact between an igneous intrusion and layers of sedimentary rock.

20) The recrystallization of unmelted material under high temperature and pressure results in

    A) Magma
    B) Sedimentary rock
    C) Igneous rock
    D) Metamorphic rock

The correct answer is D:) Metamorphic rock. The first metamorphic change is an alignment of mineral grains. Metamorphism can occur only while the rock is solid or in a plastic state (unmelted) because once the rock reaches its melting point, it becomes magma.

21) When minerals are dissolved, the resulting ions are carried in water by

    A) Precipitation
    B) Solution
    C) Suspension
    D) Evaporation

The correct answer is B:) Solution. A solution is the result of the process of dissolving.

22) If granite were exposed to intense heat and pressure, it would likely become

    A) Granite
    B) Gneiss
    C) Conglomerate
    D) Marble

The correct answer is B:) Gneiss. Granite metamorphoses into gneiss.

23) Metamorphic rock is formed in all the following ways EXCEPT

    A) Contact metamorphism
    B) Regional metamorphism
    C) Confluent metamorphism
    D) Dynamic metamorphism

The correct answer is C:) Confluent metamorphism. Contact metamorphism, regional metamorphism, and dynamic metamorphism are the three methods of forming metamorphic rock.

24) When glaciers melt and rocks and sediments of all sizes are deposited in one place it is referred to as a(n)

    A) Alluvial fan
    B) Moraine
    C) Striation
    D) Feldspar

The correct answer is B:) Moraine.

25) A rock sample is medium-grained with some recrystallization and definite foliating. It is most likely

   A) Basalt
   B) Gneiss
   C) Serpentine
   D) Schist

The correct answer is D:) Schist. Schists, the most common metamorphic rocks, are medium-grained foliated rocks that show some recrystallization and definite bands.

26) Marble and quartzite are

   A) Reterogeneous
   B) Recrystallized
   C) Multimineralic
   D) Foliated

The correct answer is B:) Recrystallized. Both marble and quartzite are homogeneous, recrystallized, monomineralic unfoliated metamorphic rocks.

27) Which of the following is NOT a result of glaciers?

   A) Moraines
   B) V-shaped valleys
   C) Striations
   D) All of the above are results of glaciers

The correct answer is B:) V-shaped valleys. Glaciers result in U-shaped valleys; rivers result in V-shaped valleys.

28) According to the rock cycle, continental crust can be created by the process of

   A) Melting
   B) Uplift
   C) Metamorphism
   D) Erosion

The correct answer is B:) Uplift. Because magma is deep inside the earth, it must be uplifted in order to ooze or spew onto the surface of the earth where it solidifies (crystallizes) to become igneous rock which forms continental crust.

www.PassYourClass.com

29) Which of the following statements is TRUE?

    A) The ocean floor is made of very light basalt and lava rock.
    B) The ocean floor is made of very dense nickel and iron.
    C) The ocean floor is made of medium density metals and sediments.
    D) The ocean floor is made of very dense basalt.

The correct answer is D:) The ocean floor is made of very dense basalt. The ocean floor is quite dense – around 3 g/cm^3.

30) According to the rock cycle, old crust is recycled by the process of

    A) Melting
    B) Uplift
    C) Metamorphism
    D) Erosion

The correct answer is A:) Melting. When rock is melted into magma again, it starts the cycle all over.

31) Bowen's Reaction Series describes

    A) The process through which a transform fault connects to a mid-oceanic ridge.
    B) The process of determining relative aging, including superposition and un-conformities.
    C) The formation of minerals as magma cools and igneous rocks form.
    D) None of the above

The correct answer is C:) The formation of minerals as magma cools and igneous rocks form. It summarizes the work of geologist Normal L. Bowen, who melted rocks and studied their properties to determine the characteristics of crystallizing minerals.

32) Igneous rock which goes through heat and/or pressure becomes

    A) Sediment
    B) Magma
    C) Sedimentary rock
    D) Metamorphic rock

The correct answer is D:) Metamorphic rock. When igneous rock undergoes heat and pressure, it becomes metamorphic rock.

33) Which of the following planets do not have surface geology?

   A) Venus, Pluto, Saturn and Uranus
   B) Jupiter, Saturn, Uranus, and Neptune
   C) Jupiter, Mars, Venus, and Neptune
   D) Mercury, Mars, Saturn, and Pluto

The correct answer is B:) Jupiter, Saturn, Uranus, and Neptune. Jupiter, Saturn, Uranus and Neptune have no surface geology because they have no solid surface.

34) Which planet has a canyon which is five times as long and four times as deep as the Grand Canyon?

   A) Mars
   B) Venus
   C) Mercury
   D) Neptune

The correct answer is A:) Mars. The Valles Marineris on Mars is a huge canyon – 4,000 km long and up to 6.5 km deep. The Grand Canyon on Earth is 804 km long and up to 1.6 km deep.

35) What climate is most conducive to chemical weathering?

   A) Cold, wet climates
   B) Cold, arid climates
   C) Hot, wet climates
   D) Hot, dry climates

The correct answer is C:) Hot, wet climates. The heat acts as a type of catalyst in speeding the chemical reactions which break down the minerals, many of which require water.

36) The planet which has a core which is the most similar to the Earth's core is

   A) Mars
   B) Venus
   C) Jupiter
   D) Mercury

The correct answer is D:) Mercury. Mercury's core is thought to be very similar to Earth's – a dense metallic, molten core surrounded by a silicate mantle and curst. The core generates a weak magnetic field.

37) The largest volcano in the solar system is on

A) Earth
B) Mars
C) Jupiter
D) Saturn

The correct answer is B:) Mars. Rising from the northern plains of Mars is Olympus Mons, the greatest volcano in the entire solar system. It is a shield volcano 600 km in diameter and 26 km high.

38) Which two planets have geysers on at least one of their moons?

A) Saturn and Uranus
B) Uranus and Neptune
C) Saturn and Neptune
D) Uranus and Jupiter

The correct answer is C:) Saturn and Neptune. Saturn's moon Enceladus has a geyser which shoots an icy plume 1,000 km into the air. Neptune's moon Triton also has geysers.

39) Which of the following is an example of chemical weathering?

A) When water gets in the cracks in rocks and freezes and expands, breaking the rock apart.
B) When acid rain interacts with the minerals in a rock and weakens its structure over time.
C) When hot temperatures cause the minerals in rocks to expand and the rock cracks.
D) When a tree grows down through the crack in a rock and pushes it apart over time.

The correct answer is B:) When acid rain interacts with the minerals in a rock and weakens its structure over time. Because the rain works on a molecular level to weaken the structure of a rock, it is a form of chemical weathering.

40) A planet which does NOT have rings is

    A) Uranus
    B) Neptune
    C) Jupiter
    D) Saturn

The correct answer is C:) Jupiter. Saturn has two sets of rings within the Roche zone. Uranus' rings are nearly elliptical and Neptune's are circular.

41) The most important agent of physical weathering in higher latitudes and altitudes is

    A) The freeze and thaw cycle
    B) Animal movements
    C) Torrential rain
    D) Strong wind

The correct answer is A:) The freeze and thaw cycle. Ice expands by about 9% of its volume, forcing open the pores and cracks in rocks. When the ice thaws, then more water can seep in than before and freeze. This cycle repeats numerous times a month in higher latitudes and altitudes.

42) Chemical weathering

    A) Changes clay into granite
    B) Can be caused by acid rain
    C) Produces exfoliation
    D) Causes minerals to crystallize

The correct answer is B:) Can be caused by acid rain. Acid rain is a weak acid formed from carbon dioxide and water, nitrogen oxide and water, or sulfur dioxide and water, all of which break rocks down as the chemicals in the rocks are dissolved by the acid or interact with the chemicals in the acid rain.

43) Chemical weathering is slowed by

    A) Tropical climates
    B) High temperatures
    C) Decaying vegetation
    D) Lack of moisture

The correct answer is D:) Lack of moisture. Decomposition is rapid when moisture and warmth are present but minimal in regions of low temperatures or low moisture.

44) Two points on the ocean floor are .5 kilometers apart and are determined to have a difference in age of 1000 years. What was the rate of sea floor spreading at the time that those portions of the ocean floor were formed?

    A) .005 kilometers per year
    B) 5 meters per year
    C) 5 centimeters per year
    D) .5 meters per year

The correct answer is C:) 5 centimeters per year. .5 kilometers = 50,000 cm. 50,000cm/1000yrs= 5 cm/yr.

45) Common minerals formed by decomposition include

    A) Granite, limestone, and gypsum
    B) Quartz grains, iron oxide, and clay
    C) Clay, sand, and mud
    D) Quartz, shale, and silica

The correct answer is B:) Quartz grains, iron oxide, and clay. New minerals formed by decomposition include clay, quartz grains, soluble forms of silica, carbonates, and limonite. Olivine, amphiboles, and pyroxene form iron oxide and soluble silica.

46) Which is NOT TRUE of loamy soils?

    A) Loamy soils feel somewhat like velvet.
    B) Loamy soils are made up of sand, clay, and silt.
    C) The particles of loamy soils do not bind together firmly.
    D) Some water can pass through loamy soils.

The correct answer is C:) The particles of loamy soils do not bind together firmly. Loamy soils (1) feel somewhat like velvet, (2) have particles that clump together, (3) are made up of sand, clay and silt, and (4) hold water but allow water to pass through slowly. The particles of sandy soils do not bind together firmly.

47) Forest type vegetation is best supported by

   A) Pedalfers
   B) Localites
   C) Pedocals
   D) Laterites

The correct answer is A:) Pedalfers. Pedalfer soils which contain large amounts of iron oxide and aluminum-rich clays form in the temperate climate of the eastern United States and support forest type vegetation.

48) The Aleutian Islands formed at which of the following geologic features?

   A) Hot spot in the mantle
   B) Divergent ocean-ocean boundary
   C) Convergent ocean-continent boundary
   D) Convergent ocean-ocean boundary

The correct answer is D:) Convergent ocean-ocean boundary. Island chains, on the other hand, form over hot spots in the mantle.

49) Which of the following is NOT a type of mass wasting?

   A) Creep
   B) Slump
   C) Hydrolysis
   D) Landslide

The correct answer is C:) Hydrolysis. Mass wasting includes the rapid movements of rock falls, slumps, rockslides or debris slides, debris flows or mudflows, and earthflows and the slow movements of creep and solufluction. Hydrolysis is the reaction of any substance with water.

50) The controlling force in mass wasting is

   A) Gravity
   B) Friction
   C) Water
   D) Wind

The correct answer is A:) Gravity. Mass wasting is the downslope movement of rock and soil under the influence of gravity.

51) A point on the ocean floor 50 kilometers from the divergent plate boundary is determined to have an age of 60 million years. What was the average rate of sea floor spreading over that time?

   A) .8 meters per year
   B) 8 centimeters per year
   C) .008 kilometers per year
   D) .08 centimeters per year

The correct answer is D:) .08 centimeters per year. 5 million centimeters/60 million years = .08 centimeters/year.

52) A reason that tropical rainforests should not be converted to agricultural uses is that

   A) Tropical land is typically pedocal soil, which is better for growing grasses
   B) There are better conditions for agriculture in mountain terracing
   C) The bedrock is too close to the surface for soil cultivation
   D) Laterite soils dry out quickly without the forest canopy, becoming brick-like

The correct answer is D:) Laterite soils dry out quickly without the forest canopy, becoming brick-like. Laterite soils, found in wet and tropical climates, allow large volumes of water to flow through them. However, they dry out quickly since the water flows through rather than being held in them. Plants that grow quickly do well in these soils; however, they need to be shaded and water must be provided daily to keep them from drying out.

53) Which of the following is a part of the continuous branch of Bowen's Reaction Series?

   A) Feldspar
   B) Biotite
   C) Amphibolite
   D) All of the above

The correct answer is A:) Feldspar. Whereas in the discontinuous branch, different types of rocks are formed, the continuous branch forms the rock feldspar with different concentrations of calcium (CA) and sodium (NA) with silicates.

54) Mass wasting is due to all the following EXCEPT

    A) Water
    B) Peer pressure
    C) Gravity
    D) One or more triggers

The correct answer is B:) Peer pressure. Mass wasting is the gravitational force influencing downslope movement of rock and soil. Water is important in the process. Water can cause pore pressure. Mass wasting usually needs one or more triggers.

55) Which of the following occurs at a convergent ocean-ocean boundary?

    A) Subduction of the older plate
    B) Collision of the two plates resulting in mountain formation
    C) Subduction of the younger plate
    D) None of the above

The correct answer is A:) Subduction of the older plate. Older ocean plates tend to be heavier and will subduct when colliding with younger, lighter plates.

56) When driving along the side of a slope you see tilted utility poles and fence posts. These are evidence of

    A) Debris flows
    B) Slump
    C) Creep
    D) Erosion

The correct answer is C:) Creep. Creep is a slow, downhill movement of soil that is usually only recognized when tree trunks appear curved or utility poles and fence posts begin to tilt.

57) As altitude increases, climatic conditions become

    A) Drier and colder
    B) Drier and warmer
    C) Wetter and colder
    D) Wetter and warmer

The correct answer is A:) Drier and colder. As altitude increases, climatic conditions become increasingly drier and colder.

58) A general characteristic of river development is

  A) Valleys tend to be deeper and narrower at the headwaters of a river
  B) Sediment load is greatest at the headwaters and decreases downstream
  C) Steep slopes lead to the development of meandering streams
  D) Wider valleys are cut at the headwaters and narrower ones downstream

The correct answer is A:) Valleys tend to be deeper and narrower at the headwaters of a river. The headwaters of a river tend to have deeper, narrower valleys that you find downstream.

59) Meanders in a stream are a result of

  A) Rapid downcutting
  B) Downcutting through sediment rather than bedrock
  C) Heavy sediment load
  D) Slow stream flow

The correct answer is D:) Slow stream flow. As a stream matures, the flow of the water slows, the stream becomes more curved and winding and forms loops known as meanders.

60) A rich habitat at the mouth of a river is called a(n)

  A) Swamp
  B) Marsh
  C) Estuary
  D) Fjord

The correct answer is C:) Estuary. A highly productive marshy habitat near the mouth of a river is called an estuary.

61) Which of the following are most likely to be temporary features of the Earth's landscape?

  A) Rivers
  B) Lakes
  C) Oceans
  D) Seas

The correct answer is B:) Lakes. In terms of geological time, lakes are considered transient and temporary.

62) An aquifer is

    A) The same as groundwater
    B) The upper surface of the zone saturated with groundwater
    C) A permeable rock formation trapped between rock layers that are impermeable
    D) The force of gravity moving water through the layers of rock and soil

The correct answer is C:) A permeable rock formation trapped between rock layers that are impermeable. An aquifer is a layer of permeable rock trapped between two layers of impermeable rock. Groundwater fills the pore spaces in the permeable rock.

63) A landscape feature created when an ice chunk melts under a layer of outwash sediment is called

    A) A kettle
    B) A moraine
    C) An esker
    D) A cirque

The correct answer is A:) A kettle. Kettles are depressions that happen when a large piece of ice becomes detached from a glacier and is covered by glacial outwash (sediment carried by meltwater streams). When the chunk of ice melts, the surface of the outwash layer sinks and the depression becomes filled with water to form a lake or pond.

64) Moraines, kettles, and bogs in the northern states of North America are remnants of

    A) Pleistocene glaciation
    B) Cenozoic glaciation
    C) Paleocene glaciation
    D) Recent glaciations

The correct answer is A:) Pleistocene glaciations. The last glaciations in the Pleistocene epoch left their evidence throughout the northern and eastern United States in the form of moraines, kettles, and bogs.

65) Which primary mineral do granite, quartz and feldspar all have in common in their compositions?

  A) Potassium
  B) Iron
  C) Nickel
  D) Silicates

The correct answer is D:) Silicates. Essentially all rocks contain silicates, which are a primary component of the earth's crust.

66) The area of a glacier where there is more melting than there is snow arriving is

  A) The percolation zone
  B) The wet snow zone
  C) The ablation zone
  D) The superimposed ice zone

The correct answer is C:) The ablation zone. At the foot or terminus of the glacier is the deposition or ablation zone where there is more melting than accumulation and the sediment is being deposited.

67) What best explains the following two statements? Some mountains located near the Earth's Equator have snow-covered peaks. Ice caps exist at the Earth's poles.

  A) High elevation and high latitude have similar effects on climate and glaciations.
  B) Both mountain and polar regions have arid climates.
  C) Mountain and polar regions receive less energy from the Sun than other regions do.
  D) An increase in snowfall and an increase in temperature have a similar effect on climate.

The correct answer is A:) High elevation and high latitude have similar effects on climate and glaciations. Continental glaciers occur in high latitudes and alpine glaciers occur in high altitudes. Both have lower temperatures due to less energy from the sun, but have increased precipitation through snowfall.

68) A landscape feature from glaciation that is one or more rounded boulders is

    A) Glacier fringe
    B) Valley train
    C) Glacial erratic
    D) Chatter mark

The correct answer is C:) Glacial erratic. Glacial erratic are rounded boulders left when a glacier melted. They may be perched on pedestals of a totally different type of rock.

69) Which of the following is NOT one of the ocean basins?

    A) Arctic
    B) Atlantic
    C) Pacific
    D) Indian

The correct answer is A:) Arctic. The three ocean basins are Pacific, Atlantic, and Indian.

70) Which of the following forms as a result of the erosion and deposition patterns of meandering rivers?

    A) Subductive lake
    B) Oxbow lake
    C) U-shaped valleys
    D) Laccoliths

The correct answer is B:) Oxbow lake. Over time the river will erode and circumvent a meandering loop, cutting it off and leaving it as a river.

71) Water in oceans tends to flow

    A) Toward the Equator
    B) From warmer to colder
    C) From an area of higher salinity to one of lower salinity
    D) Toward the north

The correct answer is C:) From an area of higher salinity to one of lower salinity. Water with a higher salinity is denser than water with a lower salinity. Water tends to flow from a denser area to a less dense area.

72) The Coriolis Effect provides evidence that the Earth

    A) Has a magnetic field
    B) Has an elliptical orbit
    C) Revolves around the sun
    D) Rotates on its axis

The correct answer is D:) Rotates on its axis. The Coriolis Effect is due to the rotation of the earth. Ocean currents generated by winds move in a clockwise direction in the Northern Hemisphere and in a counterclockwise direction in the Southern Hemisphere.

73) A wave caused by undersea volcanic action or an undersea earthquake is called a

    A) Trough
    B) Tsunami
    C) Rip tide
    D) Longshore current

The correct answer is B:) Tsunami. Seismic activity on the ocean floor, such as an earthquake or volcanic eruption, causes seismic sea waves called tsunamis.

74) Which statement best explains why Eugene, Oregon and Trenton, New Jersey, two cities with nearly the same latitude, have different climates?

    A) They are at different longitudes
    B) They are near different ocean currents
    C) They have different elevations
    D) They have different numbers of daylight hours

The correct answer is B:) They are near different ocean currents. Eugene is at a latitude of 44 while Trenton is at a latitude of 40, so their latitudes are very close. Their difference in elevation of 350 feet does not account for their differences in climate nearly as much as the difference between the Gulf Stream and the California Current.

75) A submerged flat-topped volcano is called a

    A) Continental rise
    B) Seamount
    C) Guyot
    D) Mid-ocean ridge

The correct answer is C:) Guyot. Guyots are seamounts (undersea volcanoes) that have built above sea level. Erosion by waves has then destroyed the top of the seamount resulting in a flattened shape.

76) Which of the following would NOT be a feature of a steep, rocky shore?

    A) Sea stack
    B) Marine terrace
    C) Notch
    D) Spit

The correct answer is D:) Spit. A spit is formed when a longshore current (typical of a low, gently sloping shore) drops its load of sand as it turns into a bay.

77) The amount of wind erosion depends upon

    A) Where in the world the wind is
    B) The size of the particles in the wind
    C) The height of the windbreak
    D) How flat the land is

The correct answer is B:) The size of the particles in the wind. The amount of wind erosion depends on the size of the particles being carried, the speed of the wind, the length of time the wind blows, and the resistance of the exposed rock.

78) The particles in a sand dune deposit are small and very well-sorted. They have surface pits that give them a frosted appearance. This deposit was most likely carried by

    A) Ocean currents
    B) Glacial ice
    C) Wind
    D) Gravity

The correct answer is C:) Wind. Deposits that have surface pits that give a frosted appearance have been carried by the wind.

79) Geologists have subdivided geologic time into periods based on

    A) Carbon dating
    B) Fossil evidence
    C) Rock types
    D) Landscape regions

The correct answer is B:) Fossil evidence. Because fossils actually record the slow but progressive development of life, scientists can use them to identify rocks of the same age throughout the world.

80) The San Andreas is an example of

    A) A transform fault
    B) A dip-slip fault
    C) A thrust fault
    D) An oblique-slip fault

The correct answer is A:) A transform fault. The San Andreas Fault in California is a horizontal fault along the strike which is associated with plate boundaries which makes it a transform fault.

81) Rocks react to stress in all the ways below EXCEPT

    A) Elastic deformation
    B) Plastic deformation
    C) Clastic deformation
    D) Rupture

The correct answer is C:) Clastic deformation. There are clastic sedimentary rocks but there is no such thing as clastic deformation.

82) A break in rock material with no relative movement of the rock on either side is a

    A) Fold
    B) Joint
    C) Fault
    D) Unconformity

The correct answer is B:) Joint. A joint is a break (rupture) in rock material without any relative movement of the rock on either side.

83) A person comes across a sedimentary rock formation made up of many layers of sediment. The person can determine that the layers in which position were deposited first?

    A) At the top of the formation
    B) In the middle of the formation
    C) At the bottom of the formation
    D) Cannot be determined

The correct answer is C:) At the bottom of the formation. This principle is typically applied when considering sedimentary rocks, which form layer upon layer. Each layer covers up the layer before it.

84) An anticline

    A) Will have a "U" shape
    B) Has older beds in the center
    C) Is a type of fault
    D) Will form a valley

The correct answer is B:) Has older beds in the center. An anticline is an "A" shaped fold with the older beds pushing up in the center to form a hill or ridge.

85) The boundary between the mantle and the crust is called the

    A) Mohorovicic discontinuity
    B) Asthenosphere
    C) Monorovicic disconformity
    D) Moravian orogeny

The correct answer is A:) Mohorovicic discontinuity. The boundary between the mantle and the crust is called the Mohorovicic discontinuity, or Moho.

86) A substance has decayed to 25 percent of its original amount. If it has a half-life of 1.8 billion years, how old is it?

    A) 900 million years old
    B) 2 billion years old
    C) 3.6 billion years old
    D) Cannot be determined

The correct answer is C:) 3.6 billion years old. If 25 percent is remaining then two half-lives have passed.

87) The Earth's crust

    A) Is only recycled under the oceans
    B) Is denser under the continents
    C) Increases in density with increasing ocean depth
    D) Averages 65 kilometers in depth

The correct answer is C:) Increases in density with increasing ocean depth. The Earth's crust, all of which is recycled, varies from 10 to 50 kilometers with an average of about 35 kilometers. It is thickest under continental mountains but densest under the oceans where the density increases with increasing ocean depth.

88) What other planet in this solar system is known to have active tectonic plates?

    A) Venus
    B) Neptune
    C) Mars
    D) None

The correct answer is D:) None. Although it is possible that Mars had active plate tectonics in its early history, no planets are currently known to.

89) Most earthquake damage is caused by

    A) Surface seismic waves
    B) Shear waves
    C) Primary waves
    D) Transverse waves

The correct answer is A:) Surface seismic waves. The majority of actual earthquake damage is done by the surface seismic waves.

90) Which principle allows geologists to determine the relative ages of rocks based on the fact that lower layers were deposited first?

    A) Superposition
    B) Original horizontality
    C) Unconformities
    D) Cross-cutting

The correct answer is A:) Superposition. This principle is typically applied when considering sedimentary rocks, which form layer upon layer.

91) The speed of earthquake-generated P Waves is

    A) Always faster than the S Waves
    B) The same as the S Waves
    C) Always slower than the S waves
    D) Sometimes faster and sometimes slower than S Waves

The correct answer is A:) Always faster than the S Waves. Since the P Waves travel faster than the S Waves, they arrive at the recording station first.

92) Which of the following best describes the composition of the ocean floor?

   A) Layer upon layer of various organic sediments
   B) A layer of basalt covered with other organic and inorganic sediments
   C) A layer of granite with basalt oozing up through it randomly
   D) None of the above

The correct answer is B:) A layer of basalt covered with other organic and inorganic sediments. The basalt oozes up at mid-oceanic ridges.

93) Which evidence supports the theory of ocean floor spreading?

   A) The rocks of the ocean floor and the continents have similar origins.
   B) In the ocean floor, rocks near the mid-ocean ridge are cooler than rocks near the continents.
   C) The pattern of magnetic orientation of rock is similar on both sides of the mid-ocean ridge.
   D) The density of oceanic crust is greater than the density of the continental crust.

The correct answer is C:) The pattern of magnetic orientation of rock is similar on both sides of the mid-ocean ridge. Rocks with magnetic particles align toward the magnetic poles. As the ocean floor spread, there became stripes of rocks aligned in certain ways. The stripes on one side of a mid-ocean ridge mirrored those on the other side of the ridge.

94) The deposition of large quantities of sediment in the spring and summer and smaller amounts in the fall and winter exemplifies

   A) The Law of Superposition
   B) The Principle of Uniformitarianism
   C) Strata
   D) A varve

The correct answer is D:) A varve. Any deposit that reflects a yearly cycle is a varve. Where there is annual freezing and thawing, deposits are large during spring and summer and smaller in fall and winter. Therefore, each year has two lines of deposits, one is larger than the other.

95) Fossils of the earliest plants are from the

    A) Cambrian Period
    B) Silurian Period
    C) Devonian Period
    D) Jurassic Period

The correct answer is B:) Silurian Period. The earliest plant fossils are from the Silurian Period.

96) Oxbow lakes originate as part of a(n)

    A) River
    B) Ocean
    C) Trench
    D) Glacier

The correct answer is A:) River. The meandering pattern of the river from which it originates gives an oxbow lake its curved form.

97) Joints can result from all of the following EXCEPT

    A) Extension
    B) Tension
    C) Shearing
    D) Compression

The correct answer is A:) Extension. Joints, or breaks without any movement of rock, can occur as a result of compression (squeezing together), tension (pulling apart), or shearing (pushing).

98) Vertical faults include all EXCEPT

    A) Dip-slip faults
    B) Normal faults
    C) Strike-slip faults
    D) Thrust faults

The correct answer is C:) Strike-slip faults. Vertical faults include dip-slip faults, normal faults, reverse faults, and thrust faults while horizontal faults include strike-slip faults and transform faults.

99) When a block moves vertically downward between two faults, the topographical feature that is created is a

    A) Rift valley
    B) Block mountain
    C) Angular unconformity
    D) Syncline

The correct answer is A:) Rift valley. When a block moves vertically downward between two faults, a rift valley is created.

100) A certain formation has a series of angled sedimentary layers, with horizontal layers deposited on top. The line between the two is called a(n)

    A) Tilt line
    B) Fault
    C) Angular unconformity
    D) Disconformity

The correct answer is C:) Angular unconformity. Angular unconformities are the most visual type of unconformities.

101) Mountains that were created by folding are the

    A) Alps
    B) Appalachians
    C) Andes
    D) Aral

The correct answer is B:) Appalachians. The Appalachian Mountains (from Canada to Alabama) are an example of folded mountains with long ridges and valleys in a series of anticlines and synclines formed by folded rock layers.

102) The most useful radiometric dating uses

    A) Uranium-238
    B) Carbon-12
    C) Thorium-232
    D) Potassium-40

The correct answer is D:) Potassium-40. Potassium-40 decaying to argon-40 takes 1.25 billion years but can be used on rocks as young as a few thousand years as well as on the oldest rocks known.

103) A certain rock formation has a disconformity with a fault line running through the lower half. Which of the following is NOT indicated by this?

  A) The lower half of the disconformity with a fault running through it is the oldest portion.
  B) There was a gap in time between the portions with and without the fault line.
  C) The fault must have occurred before the disconformity.
  D) There was a major environmental shift at the time of the disconformity.

The correct answer is D:) There was a major environmental shift at the time of the disconformity. Environmental shifts would characterize a nonconformity, not a disconformity.

104) Trilobites are from the

  A) Cambrian Period
  B) Devonian Period
  C) Permian Period
  D) Jurassic Period

The correct answer is A:) Cambrian Period. The earliest good fossils, trilobites and brachiopods, are from the Cambrian Period.

105) Since corals are marine animals that live in warm ocean water, how do geologists and paleontologists account for the fossil corals found in surface bedrock in areas of New York State?

  A) Corals migrated northward.
  B) Parts of New York State have migrated northward.
  C) Parts of New York State were once covered with warm ocean water.
  D) Coral-type animals once lived on land.

The correct answer is C:) Parts of New York State were once covered with warm ocean water. Whether New York has migrated farther north or not is still uncertain, but it is evident that parts of the state were covered with warm ocean water at one time.

106) Which of the following is NOT a result of subduction?

    A) Volcanic activity
    B) Trenches
    C) Mountains
    D) All of the above are results of subduction

The correct answer is D:) All of the above are results of subduction. Other features of subduction zones include island arcs and earthquakes.

107) The largest lithospheric plate is the

    A) North American
    B) Eurasian
    C) African
    D) Pacific

The correct answer is D:) Pacific. The largest plate, the Pacific Plate, includes about one-fifth of the earth's surface.

108) Which of the following does not occur when two plates collide?

    A) Subduction
    B) Convergence
    C) Rifting
    D) Transform fault

The correct answer is C:) Rifting. Crust being forced apart is a process called rifting.

109) The fact that the earth has a magnetic field is a result of

    A) Its dense, iron core
    B) Tectonic plates
    C) Oceanic currents
    D) Both A and C

The correct answer is B:) Tectonic plates. Currents in the mantle are what allow for Earth's magnetic field.

110) Which of the following mountains were formed by lava but not by a volcano?

 A) Black Hills of South Dakota
 B) Mount Etna in Italy
 C) Mount Kilimanjaro in African
 D) Hawaiian Islands

The correct answer is A:) Black Hills of South Dakota. The Black Hills of South Dakota were formed as magma tried to push its way up through the crust but failed to break the surface.

111) If gravity were the only force acting on the earth's surface, all masses of surface rock would be standing at heights determined by their thickness and the ratio of their specific gravity to that of the rocks supporting them is the principle of

 A) Uniformitarianism
 B) Seismology
 C) Isostasy
 D) Relativity

The correct answer is C:) Isostasy. The principle of isostasy states that if gravity were the only force acting on the earth's surface, all masses of surface rock would be standing at heights determined by their thickness and the ratio of their specific gravity to that of the rocks supporting them. If a mountain range erodes, the range rebounds upwards.

112) The magnetic poles of the earth

 A) Have reversed polarity several times during the earth's history
 B) Have wandered all over the earth throughout earth's history
 C) Have changed the alignment of magnetic rocks
 D) Continue to migrate, moving slightly every year

The correct answer is A:) Have reversed polarity several times during the earth's history. Although the magnetic poles do change slightly in position every year, they remain within a radius and do not wander over the Earth. However, they have reversed polarity several times during the earth's history.

113) A substance with a known half-life of 100 million years has decayed such that one-eighth of the original substance is remaining. Approximately how old is the substance?

    A) 100 million years
    B) 200 million years
    C) 300 million years
    D) 400 million years

The correct answer is C:) 300 million years. One-eighth would be the third half-life.

114) Non-living renewable resources include

    A) Metals, oil, and water
    B) Minerals, air, and water
    C) Soil, air, and water
    D) Salt, coal, and iron

The correct answer is C:) Soil, air and water. Non-living renewable resources include water, air, and soil.

115) The most important reason wetlands need to be preserved is

    A) To provide habitat for many species of wildlife
    B) To filter and clean polluted water
    C) To provide for parks and recreation
    D) To show future generations

The correct answer is B:) To filter and clean polluted water. Marshes and swamps provide a service to humans and animals by filtering and cleaning polluted water.

116) In which of the following boundaries would subduction result?

    A) Ocean-continent divergence
    B) Continent- continent transform
    C) Continent-ocean transform
    D) Ocean-ocean collision

The correct answer is D:) Ocean-ocean collision. In this case the older and denser plate would be subducted.

117) Which of the following does NOT contribute to geological erosion?

    A) Blasting mountainsides
    B) Clearing land for farming
    C) Irrigating land for farming
    D) Mining rock and ore

The correct answer is C:) Irrigating land for farming. Geological erosion is caused by blasting mountainsides for roads and dams, clearing land for farming and grazing, and mining rock and ore in quarries and strip mines.

118) The oldest rocks found on the ocean floor are approximately how old?

    A) 4 billion years
    B) 180 million years
    C) 350 million years
    D) 500 million years

The correct answer is B:) 180 million years. This is true even though the oceans are estimated to be closer to four billion years old.

119) A breakwater was built 40 years ago to protect a harbor; however, today that harbor must be dredged in order for boats to use it. What happened?

    A) Boats need deeper water today than they did 40 years ago.
    B) The ocean currents naturally change over time, causing areas that were deep to become shallower and some that were shallow to become deeper.
    C) The water level of the ocean or lake is in a shallow phase.
    D) The breakwater caused slowing of the water's motion and therefore, deposition of sand which created a sandbar.

The correct answer is D:) The breakwater caused slowing of the water's motion and therefore, deposition of sand which created a sandbar. If breakwaters are built, they cause sandbars to form in unexpected places and even contribute to the harbor not being deep enough to be a harbor after a while.

120) Acid rain can be the result of all EXCEPT the following:

    A) Volcanic eruptions
    B) Decaying vegetation
    C) Visibility degradation
    D) Fossil fuel combustion

The correct answer is C:) Visibility degradation. Acid rain and the particulate matter derivatives (sulfates and nitrates) contribute to visibility degradation.

121) The greenhouse effect is a result of which gas increasing in the atmosphere?

    A) Carbon monoxide
    B) Carbon dioxide
    C) Sulfur dioxide
    D) Nitrogen oxide

The correct answer is B:) Carbon dioxide. Carbon dioxide pumped into the atmosphere as a side effect of industry changes the balance of atmospheric gases and contributes to the greenhouse effect.

122) What type of plate boundary occurs where two plates slide past one another?

    A) Convergent
    B) Divergent
    C) Transform
    D) Transverse

The correct answer is C:) Transform. At convergent boundaries plates collides, and at divergent boundaries they pull apart.

123) Which of the following is a prominent example of a transform fault?

    A) The Himalayas
    B) San Andreas Fault
    C) Aleutian Islands
    D) African rift valleys

The correct answer is B:) San Andreas Fault. Most other transform faults are found near mid-oceanic ridges.

124) Too much ultraviolet light reaches the earth and causes skin cancers, crop damage and changes in weather when

A) Smoke stacks emit too much sulfur dioxide
B) Industrial wastes are burned
C) Freon is used as a propellant in aerosol sprays
D) Wetlands are destroyed

The correct answer is C:) Freon is used as a propellant in aerosol sprays. Freon, a propellant in aerosol sprays prior to 1978, was destroying the ozone layer and allowing too much ultraviolet light to reach the earth. When this happens, people get skin cancer more easily, crops are damaged, and changes take place in the weather and climate.

125) Oceanic crust tends to be newer than continental crust because

A) Oceanic crust subducts and is renewed faster.
B) Oceans are a fairly recent development on Earth.
C) Continental crust subducts when it meets ocean crust.
D) They aren't, continental crust dates newer than oceanic crust.

The correct answer is A:) Oceanic crust subducts and is renewed faster. This results in the age of the ocean appearing much less than it actually is.

126) The best way to dispose of industrial wastes is to

A) Seal them in steel drums and send them to the bottom of the ocean
B) Seal them with clay seals deep under the soil
C) Send them into outer space so that they are burned up re-entering the earth's atmosphere
D) Find ways to recycle and re-use as much of the wastes as possible

The correct answer is D:) Find ways to recycle and re-use as much of the wastes as possible. There presently is no best way to dispose of industrial wastes; however, any method that can recycle and re-use these wastes means that they are not a threat to civilization and that civilization is not depleting more resources and creating more toxic wastes.

127) Which material is most likely to be found 20 kilometers below sea level at the continental mountain location?

A) Granite
B) Basalt
C) Shale
D) Limestone

The correct answer is A:) Granite. Continental crust is composed of a variety of rock types, but the predominant rocks are granites which are rich in silicates.

128) The best evidence of crustal uplift would be provided by

A) Igneous rock deep within the Earth
B) Sediment in the Gulf of Mexico
C) Trenches in the Pacific Ocean floor
D) Marine fossils in the Rocky Mountains

The correct answer is D:) Marine fossils in the Rocky Mountains. Marine fossils in the Rocky Mountains provide good evidence of crustal uplift.

129) A layer of volcanic ash may serve as a time marker because

A) The ash is often a distinct color
B) The ash is generally deposited only on land
C) The ash is deposited rapidly over a large area
D) The ash is composed of index fossils

The correct answer is C:) The ash is deposited rapidly over a large area. When a volcano erupts it deposits large amounts of lava and volcanic ash over a wide area.

Test Taking Strategies

Here are some test-taking strategies that are specific to this test and to other DSST tests in general:

- Keep your eyes on the time. Pay attention to how much time you have left.

- Read the entire question and read all the answers. Many questions are not as hard to answer as they may seem. Sometimes, a difficult sounding question really only is asking you how to read an accompanying chart. Chart and graph questions are on most DANTES/DSST tests and should be an easy free point.

- If you don't know the answer immediately, the new computer-based testing lets you mark questions and come back to them later if you have time.

- Read the wording carefully. Some words can give you hints to the right answer. There are no exceptions to an answer when there are words in the question such as always, all or none. If one of the answer choices includes most or some of the right answers, but not all, then that is not the answer. Here is an example:

   The primary colors include all of the following:

   A) Red, Yellow, Blue, Green

   B) Red, Green, Yellow

   C) Red, Orange, Yellow

   D) Red, Yellow, Blue

Although item A includes all the right answers, it also includes an incorrect answer, making it incorrect. If you didn't read it carefully, were in a hurry, or didn't know the material well, you might fall for this.

- Make a guess on a question that you do not know the answer to. There is no penalty for an incorrect answer. Eliminate the answer choices that you know are incorrect. For example, this will let your guess be a 1 in 3 chance instead.

Legal Note

FLASHCARDS

This section contains flashcards for you to use to further your understanding of the material and test yourself on important concepts, names or dates. Read the term or question then flip the page over to check the answer on the back. Keep in mind that this information may not be covered in the text of the study guide. Take your time to study the flashcards, you will need to know and understand these concepts to pass the test.

Solid part of the earth's surface

Specific gravity

Igneous

Magma

Basaltic magma

Dikes

Sill

Ring of Fire

Is the weight of a mineral compared to the weight of an equal volume of water

Lithosphere

Molten rock

Formed from magma crystallization

Narrow, table-like bodies of igneous rock formed when magma entered a vertical or oblique fracture and hardened

Magma that comes directly from the mantle

Group of volcanos in the Pacific Ocean

Magma squeezes between two rock layers and hardens into a thin horizontal sheet

Caldera

Sedimentum

Clastic rocks

Nonclastic rocks

Porosity

Permeability

Precipitates

A form of limestone

Settling

Formed by the collapse of
the top of a volcano

Deposited from solution or
by organic processes

Contain fragments of
rocks, grains of minerals,
and crushed shells

Measure of the
interconnectedness of the
void spaces

Measure of the amount of
void space in a rock

Chalk

Solution occur when
chemical reactions form
a solid that settles out of
solution

Geodes

Under pressure, limestone is changed into what?

Dynamic metamorphic rock

Foliated rocks

Jupiter has how many moons?

Enceladus

Weathering

Regolith

Marble

Hollow, ball-like bodies sometimes found in limestone

Consist of compressed, parallel bands of minerals, which give the rocks a striped appearance and a layered breakage (cleavage)

Formed when rock is broken and ground with little recrystallization

Moon of Saturn

Over 60

Broken rock, soil, and loose sediment forms a primitive type of soil

The breaking down of rocks at or near to the earth's surface

Disintegration

Frost wedging

Exfoliation

Erosion

Chemical weathering

Grikes

Soil

Loamy soils

Is the cycle of thawing and refreezing

Rocks are broken down into smaller fragments without undergoing any change in chemical composition

The inclusion and transportation of surface materials by another moveable material, usually water, wind, ice or animal (including people) movements

The peeling away of the outer layers from a rock

Wide gullies in blocks of limestone

The breaking down of rocks through changes in their chemical composition

Like velvet

Part of the surface zone that has been altered by weathering, erosion and the processes of breakdown that include microbes and decay

Pedalfers

Laterites

Mass wasting

Slumps

Creep

Peneplain

Floodplains

Estuary

Red-orange soils rich in iron and aluminum oxides

Contain large amounts of iron oxide and aluminum-rich clays, making the soil a brown to reddish brown color

Involve a mass of soil or soil and other materials sliding along a curved, rotational surface

The downslope movement of rock and soil under the influence of gravity

"almost a plain"

A slow, downhill movement of soil

An area formed at the mouth of a river where river currents interact with ocean tides

The flat areas on both sides of a mature river or stream

Permeable rocks filled with water

Spring

Stalagmite

Stalactite

Glacier

Sinkholes

Till

Drumlin

Groundwater that flows out from underground onto the surface

Aquifers

Icicle-like structures of calcium carbonate that hang from the roofs of caves

Is built by water falling on a constant spot on the cave floor and evaporates leaving a deposit of calcium carbonate

Funnel-shaped depressions created by dissolved limestone

Large, slow-moving river of ice, formed from compacted layers of snow

Oval-shaped mound of till

When glaciers melt and retreat and leave behind piles of unsorted rock debris